Where the
River Reigns

Tim,
   I hope you
will enjoy my
stories from our
cabin in Alaska.
Happy Father's Day!

B

Where the
River Reigns

*One man's dream for a log cabin
in the Wild of Alaska*

Brian P. Horacek

Publisher:
Clear Creek Publications –
A division of Clear Creek Holdings, Corp.

Mill Creek, Washington
info@ClearCreekPub.com
http://ClearCreekPub.com

Cover and text design:	Kris Cotterman- Exodus Design www.exodusdesign.com
Proofreader:	Sherrill Carlson
Photos:	Brian Horacek (unless noted)
Map Art:	Talkeetna Chamber of Commerce, www.talkeetnachamber.org
Sketch Art:	Brian Horacek, Adrienne Horacek, & Jaeden Horacek
Printer:	Bang Printing

Copyright 2008 by Brian Horacek
1st edition

Printed in the United States of America
ISBN Print Edition:	978-0-9802360-3-3
ISBN PDF Screen Edition:	978-0-9802360-0-2
ISBN eBook Edition:	978-0-9802360-2-6

Dedication

This book is dedicated to my dad, Charles J. Horacek. May his soul rest in the new peace that passes all understanding, free from pain and worry. He made the incredible investment of his time, allowing his children the opportunity to learn about the outdoors. He shared his experiences and taught us the essence of appreciating all that God has made for our enjoyment.

And for those who share in the dream of having their piece of "paradise," whereever that may be, may you, too, one day realize your dream as my dad did.

Acknowledgments

I have been truly blessed to have the privilege of sharing this story of my dad and some of the more meaningful experiences in his life. I am forever grateful to my parents for their love over the years. They taught me to appreciate this beautiful world. They took the time to teach me the skills and talents I have.

Mom spent many hours sketching scenes for the chapter headings. I am grateful for her talent and the creativity she shared to help make this possible.

My wife has been so patient and supportive over the years. I would not have been able to do this without her love.

My son Jaeden and daughter Talia for their patience and understanding when I was not able to give them the time or attention I would normally have while writing this book. They are my inspiration and purpose in life.

–B.P.H.

Contents

Introduction

This is a narrative of the many experiences I have had at our family cabin in Alaska. In the fall of 2005, I approached my dad with the idea of this book. He was in the battle of his life with cancer and I knew he probably would not survive much longer.

One evening during one of the many regular calls we had, I told my dad about my desire to write a book. He commented, "That's great, what are you going to write about?" I replied, "Dad, I would like to write a book about you and the cabin." He said softly and nonchalantly, "That'll be neat."

We made some time over the next few weeks to discuss the book together. I told him about the many questions I had and we began to make the initial plans. It was my intention to write this book with him. Unfortunately I would not have that privilege. A few weeks after our discussions, he was admitted to the hospital for complications with pain from shattered vertebrae. He never left the hospital.

This work is the culmination of that beginning. It is my intention to share the over 30 years of experiences we had together as a family in finding, planning, building, and experiencing life with a log cabin in the Alaska wild. My dad was passionate in his own way about spending time away from the city and experiencing all that nature had to offer. He was never inhibited by the challenges that it took to achieve that end. To the contrary, I think it made it even more of an adventure for him. Despite weather or mechanical difficulties, he was persistent in making sure he and his family were able to experience this lifestyle choice. After all, we all have choices in how we want to spend our resources and time.

There were many times that plans to get to our cabin were thwarted for one reason or another. My dad was never deterred by any of these. If he had a motor that was not working, he would find a way to fix it. If he couldn't fix it himself, he would find someone else who could. If they couldn't fix it, he would break down and buy a new one.

When it came time to start taking the family to the property he had found, he was no longer in a position to rely on someone else. Like many of his contemporaries, he made plans to build his own boat rather than buying something new. This was the practical thing for a man with a young family and its many expenses.

My dad was a talented engineer and there wasn't anything he couldn't build or fix. He didn't know how to build a log cabin but he figured it out, along with how to have heat, light, and water when there were no utilities available at such a remote place.

Over the years he figured out how to build better and better boats, big enough and with enough horsepower to bring a family of seven, with all the required gear and essentials, up a river to the cabin. He loved to fish and spend time tinkering with things at the cabin. It wasn't until I became a father that I understood why. This was his escape, his break from the fast-paced, routine-driven life many of us find ourselves living.

My dad valued his time at the cabin and made it a priority in his life and ours. Even more he valued sharing this with others, friends as well as family. It is through these experiences, one could say, that he found his ministry in life. I don't think he would have ever seen it that way. To him it was just doing what was natural. He was following his passion in life and just wanted others to partake. In hindsight I can see how this had such an impact on the many people who shared these experiences with him. My dad's life touched so many people.

He is greatly missed but never will be forgotten.

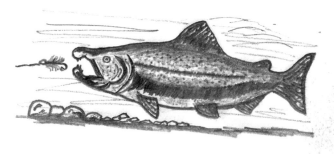

Chapter 1
Quest for Kings

Quest (k west) n. (< L. quaerere, seek)
1. a seeking; hunt
2. a journey for adventure.
- Webster's New World Dictionary

It was shortly after midnight when our plane touched down in Anchorage. Jim leaned over and looked out the window commenting on how light it was still. A Seattle native, he had never experienced the late summer nights of Alaska. I smiled and said "You can fish all night for kings if you want." Jim was one of three friends joining me this trip. My friend Buz was also along with a friend and colleague of his named Josh. Buz had made this trip the previous year and was eager to return.

Buz and Josh met Jim and me in Seattle. They made the short hop up from the Vancouver, Washington area. Josh is a computer programmer and Buz an entrepreneur in The Dalles, Oregon. Jim is a neighbor and friend of mine from the Seattle area where he is a well respected and decorated police officer. Neither Buz nor Jim had met before so this was set to be an interesting trip.

It was early July when the weather is usually quite warm, at least by Alaska standards. No real rain was in sight over the mountains to the east or to the north towards McKinley, the direction we would eventually be heading. After a short night of sleep at Mom and Dad's house and a nice home-cooked breakfast, it was off to the grocery store to stock up for our trip. One of the things you learn over the years of boating on rivers is that weight is a constant enemy. Dad was always aware of how much weight we were going to have with us in the boat. He had the ability to calculate in his head how much weight our food and gear would weigh and if we were going to have to take more than one or two trips in the boat. Dad always led by example in this area. It didn't matter if we were going to be gone for a day or week. When it was time to go, he had a bag of things the size of a small gym bag. That was it. I always felt guilty having more stuff than that. It was always entertaining to see the look on Dad's face when our out-of-state guests showed up with three large duffel bags each.

Dad, Jim, Buz, and Josh ready to go catch some kings

After shopping we began the ritual of packing and loading the vehicles. There were the four of us from Washington, my Dad, Mom, and my brother Scott. One of my sisters, Carrie, would follow with her son in a few days. With this many people, even a large Suburban can fill up quickly. My brother planned on driving his Expedition to help balance out our large load of food, gear, and people. This made it possible for us to take both boats. Gas was the only missing ingredient before our trek north. We made a last stop on our way out of town to get fishing licenses and beer and spirits for the long summer nights ahead.

The drive would take us north on the Glenn Highway until we reached the turnoff for the George Parks Highway. The Parks Highway took us north towards Mount McKinley National Park and Fairbanks. We finally turned right and exited on the Talkeetna Spur road towards the town of Talkeetna. Drive time would be about two and a half hours out of Anchorage. Along the way is some of the prettiest country you could ever see. With the Chugach Mountains to our right and the Talkeetna Mountains in front of us to the north, one feels small within these large, vast, surroundings. We would cross no fewer than 10 major rivers and creeks along the way to our destination, passing through many small Alaskan towns like Wasilla, Willow, and Houston. Conversation on the ride was centered on the upcoming fishing trip for king salmon and of course the never-eventless boat ride up the river.

Talkeetna is a small town of approximately 350 inhabitants in the interior of south central Alaska. Located 120 miles north of Anchorage, it is rich with history. The Alaska Railroad runs directly through the town on its way north to Fairbanks. In 1915 President Woodrow Wilson selected the town as the site for the Engineering Commission Headquarters for the construction of the Alaska Railroad.

In 1892 gold was discovered on the Susitna River. By 1896, Talkeetna was established and was a busy trading post and mining town by 1910.

Talkeetna served as major staging grounds for supplies carried up the river by steamship. The town's history reaches back much further than that. The Den'aina Indians, an Athabascan Indian subgroup, were the first to inhabit the upper Cook Inlet drainage area and established villages in what is now the area of Talkeetna. They were known for their resourcefulness, independence, and resistance to the change encroaching on their territory by persistent new Russian traders who were interested in expanding their own pockets and trade.

Athabascan Indians have many beautiful crafts that have been passed down through the centuries. Some can now be found in many of the various small shops filled with Alaskan art and crafts in Talkeetna. I encourage anyone who stops in town to visit every shop as they are all different and unique in their own way. Each holds treasure from Alaska waiting to be found. A small public park is near the center of town which is home to the annual Moose Dropping Festival.

Talkeetna is also known by an elite brotherhood around the world as the major jumpoff for climbers leaving to make their mark on history by climbing the tallest mountain in North America, Mount McKinley, also known as "Denali," the original Athabascan name.

When we arrived at the turn off, the final hill that begins our descent into town boasts one of the most spectacular views of the Alaska Range and all its glory. Mount McKinley, 20,320 feet, is anchored by Mount Foracker, 17,400 feet tall, and Mount Hunter, 14,573 feet. We stop, like many of the other tourists, at a small pull out on the highway. I have seen this sight dozens of times over the years and never get tired of another opportunity to see it again, offering a breathtaking view for our out-of-state guests. After a few pictures it's on to the town and the boat launch.

Beautiful view of the Alaska Range in the distance

Talkeetna is nestled against one of the largest river confluences in Alaska. The mighty Susitna River flows due south to the Cook Inlet, one of the many waterways Captain Cook explored on his voyages. The town of Talkeetna is at the confluence of the Talkeetna, Chulitna, and Susitna River. The Den'aina Indians named the Susitna River which means "sand island river," the Chulitna River which means "river of big leaf trees," and the Talkeetna, meaning "river of plenty." Most know the town for its newer Alaskan meaning of "where three rivers meet."

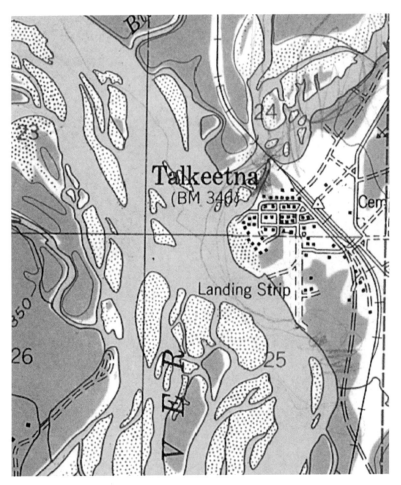

This map shows the sheer size of the Big Susitna River after the Chulitna and Talkeetna have joined its confluence and the location of the town of Talkeetna. Each square represents a square mile. Notice the many fingers or channels.

If you are not from Alaska and have never had the opportunity to see a large river like the Talkeetna, it would be hard to imagine the setting. These rivers are massive, milky gray highways of running water. The milky color is due to the high levels of silt from the glaciers were they originated. If you were to scoop a cup of water out of the river it would appear to have sand floating around in it, not very appealing to drink. These rivers carry a huge volume of water at a very high velocity, carving their way through the landscape as they have for thousands of years.

There are points where there are so many fingers that the river stretches out for over a mile in width. The bottom of the river is mostly small-size river rock and areas filled with silt. Large sand bars that look like a beach line the sides of the river as do countless fallen, washed-up trees. Many of these sand bars are actually "rock bars" made of small, gravel-size rock on up to basketball-size river rock. The number of colors and textures of the stone are seemingly infinite. No two rocks look alike. One of my favorite pastimes as a young boy was to spend hours walking the rock bars in search of that perfect rock or unique piece of driftwood. One of the rarest finds and most prized was finding a large bald eagle feather. I have several that I have found over the years.

The boat launch is always an exciting place to be. It marks the end of the road trip and the beginning of the water trip. Dad was always glad when the motors started without too much work and we were able to get on our way after loading. This trip we brought both boats. One is a light aluminum, canvas-green sled with a Johnson 80 horse power outboard jet on an electric hydraulic lift. The other newer and larger boat is a silver-colored sled with a blue canopy cover. There are cushioned seats to sit on, and room for more gear. It is powered by a Johnson 120 horse power outboard jet.

The author with Mom and Dad

The reason for bringing both boats is very simple. If the water is too low, we will not be able to get up the creek to our cabin with the larger of the two boats. Suffice to say we wanted to make sure we could get where we wanted to go, no matter what the water conditions were like. Dad is "chief captain" of the larger boat and my brother Scott has taken over piloting the smaller.

My brother Scott with our loaded second boat

We had hoped to make it up in one trip but much to my Dad's chagrin we had just too much weight.

My mom and Josh stayed behind with some of the gear while I left with Dad and Jim in the larger boat and Buz with Scott in the smaller.

Scott piloting up the Talkeetna

The river is an awesome force of nature. As a young boy, my dad taught me how to fully appreciate and respect its force. Hip waders or hip boots as we always called them, were a necessary evil in and around the river. My dad never did like them because of the false sense of security one has with them on. Dad always felt that there was never a reason to wade any deeper than knee high. It is very easy to underestimate the power of the river with its swift current and varying types of bottom and bed. One wrong step and you could be swept into the channel. The real problem with this is not the fact that you have just fallen in the river; it is the fact that your hip boots have now filled with water and act as an extra weight strapped to your legs which can not be taken off. When the water fills your boots it also creates a suction actually sticking to your legs. Those of you who have tried taking your waders off after getting even a small amount of water over the edge understand the concept at point. For this reason I never traveled in the boat with my waders pulled up and fastened to my pants. One of those little lessons learned early in life around the river.

Heading up the river

There simply is not a better feeling than cruising up a river. The wind and spray in your face is enough to make any man smile like a child in a candy store. To the left of us is a beautiful sight of Mount McKinley towering over the tops of the surrounding mountains. The air is sweet from the smell of the cottonwood trees and beautiful green foliage covers the river's banks. Bald eagles can be seen soaring high above or perched on a tree branch on the side of the river. Moose and bear can also be seen on occasion along the riverbank. Exhilaration runs through your veins as we make our way upstream to our final destination, the Horacek cabin.

Chapter 2
Clear Creek

Chunilna Creek – The original Athabascan name given to this creek. Chunilna Creek flows directly out of the hills to the south of Denali and the Alaska Mountain Range. There are still many actively worked gold mines in operation on the creek today.

The boat ride is 6 miles upstream and a short 30 minutes on a good day. There are many factors though that can affect that time period. Four miles up the Talkeetna River we take a left up a creek called Clear creek. This creek is more like a river to someone other than an Alaskan. As we traveled up the river and came to the mouth of the creek we had to slow to a crawl in order to not make much of a wake for the people fishing. Once past them, it is back to full power in order to stay on the step and avoid hitting the rocks. The creek had recently changed its channels and was cutting a new main channel through the trees. As a result, the maneuvering was quite tricky for a boat. Dad has had much experience running this river but with this new channel it was dangerous even to an experienced river captain.

We were safe navigating the first few twists and turns, in and out of fallen trees and newly formed rock bars. As we approached a spot that I knew could cause a problem, my stomach tensed. It was going to be a 45-degree turn north, between a few very large cottonwood trees that had newly fallen. They were directly across the river blocking all the ways through the last weekend my dad and brothers were there. They had to use a chainsaw to cut through a tree with about a four-foot diameter. The tough part was the need to cut through the tree on both sides in order to free it to float away and unblock the channel. With that completed, they were able to make it up the creek and to the cabin. This trip we were not as lucky. Directly after swerving to miss a tree we ended up on the rock bar. There was a new tree blocking most of the creek and making passage impossible. Dad was forced to run the boat aground. My brother was following close behind and was able to pull over in time to avoid the same problem.

It was a warm day and normally I would be wearing a pair of hip waders. This day I was in shorts and wearing a pair of sandals. I was on the opposite side of the creek from the tree and my brother who at this time had already retrieved the chain saw from his boat and begun cutting the tree at its base. The tree did not want to let go with out a fight. I waded the current and climbed up on the end that was pointing down stream and began to bounce the tree up and down in the water. Luckily I have good balance and was able to keep myself from being thrown into the water. As the tree began to finally break loose I had to jump off towards the other side of the creek and hope I would land close to the gravel bar and not be swept down the creek. The tree broke loose and floated away successfully without incident. I was only wet up to my waist and safe on the gravel bar. With a quick shove back into the current we were on our way.

View of the creek below the cabin

The water flattened out to a wide area in the creek. The boat cut through it like butter compared to the battle through the many shallows and rapids down stream. I knew we were there. Ahead in the distance on the left side of the creek I could see the roof of our cabin. Within a few seconds we were slowing to a complete stop. My job, as it has been since I was old enough to do it, was to jump off the bow of the boat and tie up for Dad. He was very conscious of always leaving the motor idling just enough in case the rope did not hold. The second part of my job was to then walk up the bank of the creek to the cabin with the shotgun to make sure all was clear and there were no uninvited guests of a furry nature.

It had been one full year since I had been there last. The sight, the smell, the memories came flooding back in an instant.

I realized how much I absolutely loved this place. One of the thrills was bringing someone there who had never experienced a trip like this. I knew Jim and Josh were in for a thrill of a lifetime and was happy Buz was able to join me again this year. Dad opened the cabin, always with his special tool and hidden lock on the door to help keep out any unwanted visitors.

View of the front of the cabin when we arrived

We began the ritual of carrying all the gear up the short trail to the cabin. Some went into the cabin; some was left out on the front porch area. There was no doubt we were going to be crowded this trip. Dad was then on his way back down the creek for his second trip to pick up the remaining passengers and gear. I always was very nervous when my dad would venture on his own in the boat especially now with him being a bit older and not quite as quick with his reactions as he once was.

We all took some time to get settled in and fix some lunch. Buz was in a hurry as usual to get down to the creek to do some fishing. Jim was right behind him. There is something I have to tell about this special place at this point of our story. This creek is the most beautiful crystal clear water you have ever seen. To top it off, it happens to have every species of salmon in it at some point during the summer months. In addition to salmon, there is an abundance of Rainbow Trout, Artic Grayling, and Dolly Varden. A literal fishing paradise, depending on the weather. Weather always plays a key role with everything in Alaska. It dictates whether you can come or go, be inside or out, and be safe or not. We happened to pick the right time of year this trip as we had planned on fishing for kings! The weather could not have been better. It would reach the 80's during the day and stay in the 60's at night. This is normally warmer than I would like for fishing but I was not about to complain. With weather like this we were able to fish in nothing but waders and shorts. No shirt was required but a lot of sun block was certainly necessary as the long hot days can be torture to your skin. Sunglasses were definitely a must as the reflection off the water was quite strong. With polarized lenses you are able to see the salmon quite well in the water. The year before was a blast as I was able to watch my friend Buz catching every species of salmon in one trip. Not all of them were worth catching but none-the-less fun for me to watch.

One of the most memorable experiences from that last trip was watching Buz talk on his cell phone telling his wife he had just caught a king salmon with his hands! You may think this is one of those tall fish tales. I was there and have the picture to prove it. Let's say this poor salmon was on the last leg of his long trip up the creek from the ocean. Salmon become quite lethargic and slow as they start to approach the end of their life cycle after spawning. This particular fish happened to be quite close to the bank were Buz was standing enabling him to act quickly to grab the salmon from behind and pick him up out of the water by the tail. He released him after I had taken a photo to document the moment.

The evening was filled with talk and laughter around the campfire pit. Campfire time is actually the best time of the trip to the cabin as everyone has time to talk about the day and share stories and jokes. There was no lacking of either with Buz and Jim together. Buz is a very accomplished guitar player and singer but what he is really known for is, "his gift of gab." Take this and add a little sarcastic humor and you are basically entertained for the night.

Campfire time

The funny thing is that Buz and Jim did not know each other. They had both heard about each other through their wives. Jim's wife owns a salon and Buz's wife had worked with her at one time. I never thought Buz would meet his match when it came to talk but Jim had him at every turn and corner. This made for an especially amusing time around the campfire. Dad thought it was all just as fun as it could be. He would sit in his favorite chair, manning the fire and a cocktail. The strange thing about being out in the wild in Alaska during the summer months is that you never really know what time it is. Dinner was usually not served until around 8 p.m. We were usually up talking until well after midnight while it was still light out. This did have a tendency to make things a little tough on your biological clock.

Dad with my brother's dog

Day one for fishing was met with mixed results, as the newcomers were working on their tactics and form. I was able to reel in a nice 25-pounder, a little on the small side as the average goes. After our fun and fishing we called it a day. The kings were obviously not this far up the river yet. We would try our luck downstream tomorrow.

Over the next few days we had much success in fishing, as everyone was able to catch the elusive king salmon. I was fortunate enough to catch what was close to my all time largest. We had ventured downstream to a hole that I knew would produce good results. I had a king hooked after being there only a few minutes. It would start to run and I could not stop it and twang!! The line would snap. This happened three or four times before I finally got frustrated fishing with my medium weight rod and 20-lb. test line. Jim was taking a break at this point and I borrowed his rig to see if I could finally catch something. The water where we were fishing had a very strong current that was just above a wide shallow bar in the river.

I was fishing on the west side with my left arm upstream. I could see the kings schooled up in front of me. I had been here before and knew exactly how to place my lure. There was one king that stuck out more than all of the rest. He was a little redder in color. King salmon start to turn from a bright shiny silver color to a red color when they enter the fresh water of the rivers to spawn. This particular salmon caught my eye because it had a bright pink lure stuck in its back! Now, you may be wondering why this fish had a lure in it. Well, this is the sign of a very strong fish. Someone at some point had hooked this fish and lost the battle. To me this represented a challenge. All my attention was centered on this one fish, even though there were many others around it. Within a few strategically placed casts I was able to hook this monster! Now, I am not a large man by any means. I am tough though, and had been in this position before. I knew what this fish was going to do. He made a few giant leaps out of the water trying to spit the lure and then headed downstream. It was at that point I knew I was in for a fight. Buz and Josh were on the other side of the river directly across from me. They were frustrated at this point for not catching anything and here I was with my fourth king in less than an hour. Jim on the other hand was having fun watching me loose fish and all the while taping me on his video camera.

When this fish came on, he knew it was a different situation as I had a heavier rod and reel. The strain on my arms and hands was tremendous. I cannot tell you how hard it is to fight a large king salmon with the swift current of a river. You feel like you are not only fighting the fish but that the river is somehow on the side of the salmon to aid and abet in its success. This is part of the "thrill and the kill." Yes, kill, as though you don't plan on eating the salmon you would like to catch. I have no patience for those that feel this is somehow an unfair sport. This fish had the better of me and he knew it. This is the moment that I live for. I did not travel 2,000 miles to not catch a big fish. This is a ritual for me on an annual basis. Feeling the pressure of all of my friends that I had brought, I calmly fought the fight. They had seen me loose the previous three fish I had hooked so at this point there was not much attention being paid. They saw me having to walk down the side of the river in order to keep from loosing this fish. Once a king gets the turn on you and starts his run downstream, all you can do is hold on. There is no reel or rod that is going to hold him.

Fifteen minutes had gone by and this fish had drug me a good hundred yards downstream. At this point I was now invading other fishermen's space. This is not a problem with fishing etiquette in Alaska, assuming you are from Alaska. It is expected that you give access to the one with the fish on. Luckily the people below were quite understanding and willing to move their lines out of the way as I followed my salmon down the river. Below the rapids I had to cross in order to keep this fish, lay another set of rapids, once there I knew I could not keep a fish from winning.

My strategy changed as soon as we crossed the rapids and were in calmer water. I began to pull hard on the rod to turn the nose of the fish upstream. Once I was able to do this, it was only a matter of time to tire him out. Another 20 minutes went by as people watched me reel this beast in. Once I landed him, I was able to see his massive size. Red as he was, he was in quite good fighting shape. We estimated his weight to be around 50 pounds. He had a large hooknose and large teeth. I pulled the lure that was stuck in his back and put it in my hat as a trophy. He also had another lure in his mouth. This was a true warrior of a fish.

There are not many fish in my lifetime that I can say had my true respect for their sheer will to live and fight until the end. Everyone caught fish that day and made the trip downstream a big success.

(above) My big king   (bottom left) Jim   (bottom right) Buz

Chapter 3
Midnight Sun

"The sky is the daily bread of the eyes."
-Ralph Waldo Emerson

As the Earth orbits around the Sun, its tilt makes the North Pole face toward the Sun in the summer months, allowing the sun to be seen even along the Artic Circle just touching the horizon, never setting on June 21st, Summer Solstice. The further north one is, the more dramatic the sight.

Upon our return to the Horacek hacienda, Dad was only mildly impressed, as much as I wanted him to say "that's a beauty," he only looked and smiled like it was no big deal. He had seen many big fish in his day. Dad was at a point in his fishing career that he didn't need to venture down stream to catch a fish. He preferred to stay in camp and simply walk 15 feet to the creek, and throw a line in when he pleased. He knew there were more fish in the creek right in front of the cabin than anywhere else.

That night we had much salmon to clean and process. My sister Carrie is the expert on filleting fish. Somewhere along the way she learned better than us boys how to fillet fish. So, when she had arrived and caught fish within an hour of arriving, the guys were forced to contend with her. Carrie was able to help with all the filleting which is the first important step in smoking salmon.

We found that using a table with leg extensions right at the waters edge is the most efficient method. This makes it much easier on the back and allows the scraps to be thrown directly in the creek for the gulls to eat. A small piece of an old door mat helps hold the slimy fish in place while cutting.

Me and Carrie preparing to fillet a king salmon

Salmon is actually best when fresh and smoked. Dad has a secret recipe that he has used for 30 years. Once the salmon is prepared it is put into the brine which is a mixture of brown sugar, molasses, and other key ingredients. It is then soaked over night to absorb the brine. Then the salmon is patted dry and placed into the smoker to smoke and cook for 8 hours or so. Once cooked with smoke and heat the salmon is removed from the smoker and placed on racks to cool and dry.

Dad preparing salmon for the smoker

My dad was a clever guy and had made a smoker out of an old refrigerator. The bottom was removed and replaced with a small hibachi grill. On the grill we burned small pieces of alder. This tree is famous for its smoke and odor. Alder happens to be very prevalent around our cabin. One must cut the alder into small pieces that burn easily and create a lot of smoke. This takes a lot of patience and attention. My dad is a specialist at this. He prides himself at making sure all is going well with the smoking. That night we would feast on fresh salmon and shrimp on the fire pit grill.

Jim and I preparing shrimp on the grill while Dad oversees

One evening Jim and I were the last two awake and left to manage the fire pit. It was our turn to "burn some midnight oil" as dad would say. We were on "official salmon smoking duty." Basically we were to make sure the salmon which had been left out to dry was then placed in a closed space to ensure its safety from the large furry creatures that inhabit the area. Jim and I had a great time talking and sharing stories.

It was shortly after 2:30 a.m. when we heard a loud yell from the hill up above us. My sister Carrie and her son Anthony had been inside their cabin, trying to get to sleep, when they saw a black bear walking below their window. Jim and I immediately jumped to attention. I went into the cabin to wake my brother Scott and get the shotgun. He asked me if the bear was outside the cabin and I replied "No, but it was up near Carrie's." He proceeded to roll over, irritated at having been awakened, and went back to sleep. I checked with my sister that she was all right on the two-way radio. I proceeded to walk up to my sister's cabin, which was a few hundred yards north of us. The walk was a straight shot past the sauna and then straight up a hill. This hill is steep. You have to make every effort to place your step in order to make it up the hill. At the top lay a trail that ran north a short distance to the cabin. The bear had made his way past the cabin and disappeared into the woods deciding to avoid coming down our way.

Jim and I decided that now would be a good time to put the racks of fish in the sauna where they would be safe for the night. I think there was also something to that decision that was a bit self serving, neither of us wanting to continue to remain sitting in the dark with fish lying around. We then retired for the evening.

Mornings come early in Alaska in the summer so I value the little amount of sleep I get. Sleeping arrangements with six men and my mom were a challenge in our cozy cabin. Mom has her own sleeping quarters in a small loft at the back of the cabin.

Mom's sleeping loft in top of the back of the cabin complete with a privacy curtain

There were bunk beds that slept two, a cot that could be utilized and a large upper loft sleeping area over the front porch. The challenge was not the beds but the noises that follow. I have never been a heavy sleeper. My ears are tuned to every sound around me while I try to drift away into the sleep zone. Since I was a boy, I have always had a difficult time sleeping in the woods. My mind would race from one frightening bear dream to another. I would hear every twig crack outside my tent or cabin. I could hear changes in the water flow of the creek as it raced over the rocks. Footsteps of the critters that live around were a normal sound in the night. Most animals tend to be more nocturnal and were always more active at that time. As you could imagine, this was not an easy thing for me to overcome. My dad tended to be quite a sound sleeper. I however take after my mother. This meant that I felt obligated as the eldest son to be "on guard" for my family while they slept. I am sure there are plenty of professional explanations out there amongst the psychiatric community about that. Nonetheless I have learned to live with it just fine. That is of course until nights like this. As I lay in my sleeping bag, staring at the wood ceiling, I counted no less than five different snore tones being belted out like professional operatic snorers. I tell you it was enough to vibrate the log rafters and metal roofing.

View into the upper front loft sleeping area complete with mosquito netting

I was up in the front loft. This has been my designated sleeping spot for many years. It does sleep two or three if needed. My bunkmates were Buz and Jim who were heavily adding to the "log sawing symphony." Sawing logs is probably more descriptive than the operatic vocalist comparison. It was definitely closer to the sound of buzzing chainsaws. As one who is a light sleeper, this was a nightmare. I did however come prepared for this exact problem. My handy earplugs I use for things like shooting my guns should have done the trick. Unfortunately they did not work as well as I had planned. This called for more drastic measures. I changed where I would be sleeping. I was not going to endure another night of this torture and it was off to my sister's cabin up on the hill far away from "Snoredom."

The following evening we had a great time around the campfire. By this time in the trip we had not showered for several days and began to smell a little on the foul side, or I should say salmon side. One of the incredible luxuries we had at the cabin was the sauna. I plan on going into more detail about this in a subsequent chapter. For the time being, I wanted to share a very memorable story that happened on "Sauna Night." Sauna night is a ritual when visiting the cabin for more than two days. It typically would take a good hour of stoking the fire to get the sauna to the optimal temperature of about 130°F.

There is nothing better than the feeling you have after a great sauna. We usually can sit in the sauna for 15 minutes or so before needing some air to cool for a few minutes then returning back for more heating and sweating. The sauna can easily hold four to five adults. This particular round was Jim and I, my brother Scott and my nephew Anthony. One of the long-held traditions for our family was taking a sauna and running down to the river in the buff as fast as you can and jumping in the freezing water. This is not for the faint of heart. I had performed this ritual since I was a kid.

Josh and Jim stunned from the cold creek followed by me and my nephew Anthony

For newcomers and guests at the cabin, this was a true test of their manliness. It simply was not an option to not do it. That is unless you wanted to be on cooking duty and dishes duty the whole trip. This night was not going to be a problem as all had agreed to the ritual dipping in the creek. It was quite refreshing. All of the impurities that had made their way to the surface were washed away in one fell swoop. My nephew was 14 at the time and at the age when nothing can seem to harm you. Once was never enough. After we all had made a quick trip and back, Anthony wanted to go again. I reluctantly agreed. You can read what happened next when you get to the chapter 14, Bear Tales II!

Bare buns running back to the warmth of the sauna

Each trip made to the cabin always involves some work even though we were primarily there for fishing. Dad had spent a weekend cutting boards for some new steps that would make it easier for him to get down to the waters edge. He had the misfortune of breaking the heel of his foot many years ago and it is difficult to climb the steep bank.

My brother Chris putting the finishing touches on the new steps

Our trip grew to an end and we were all reluctant to leave. I was especially sensitive to the fact that my dad was not getting younger and it was getting harder and harder for him to make the trek to the cabin. I never knew when or if it would be my last trip with him. We all made plans for the next year to come back and go for the silvers in August. Little did I know that this was my last trip to the cabin with my dad.

The crew after returning to Anchorage for the flight back to Seattle, Buz, Scott, Jim, Me, Dad, & Josh

Alaska
N

Chapter 4:
North to Alaska

"Hitch your wagon on a star"
-Ralph Waldo Emerson

Charles (Chuck) Jacob Horacek, my dad, was born June 29th, 1939, in Norfolk, Nebraska to the son of an immigrant from Czechoslovakia. His dad's name was Ladislav Anthony Horacek but his friends called him Jake for short. His dad and brother came to this country to start a better life for themselves and their families. They ended up in the retail business and owning two banks, both of which were lost during the Great Depression. Dad grew up spending time in Fremont and then later in Omaha, Nebraska.

Jake was married to Martha and was in the grocery business and worked for the local Hinky Dinky market. He was a hard worker with a solid middle class value system. Dad had two older brothers Perry and Jerry, and a younger brother Pete. Perry went to school at Oklahoma State University and Jerry to the Naval Academy in Annapolis. Dad was a handsome young man, with a stocky build and excelled at football in high school in Omaha. Dad later went into the Army Reserves and followed his older brother Perry to Stillwater where he too attended college at Oklahoma State University. Unlike Perry who was in the architecture school, dad chose to study civil engineering. It was through one of his college professors who helped him land a summer job that dad was able to get his first experience in the forty-ninth state of the union, Alaska.

Dad went to Alaska to work on one of the many state highway projects that were going on in the early 1960's. It is here that the seed was planted of one day experiencing Alaska on a permanent basis. He worked hard on his job and was able to find spare time trying his hand at fishing in many of the streams along the path of the project. This one trip laid the foundation of what would come to pass many years later.

Dad 1961

Dad met my mother, Lucul Adrienne Stone, at school in Stillwater. Like many college students then, they married in their senior year. Mom came from a very well-established family in Tulsa, Oklahoma. Her grandfather was one of the original founders of the first major oil refinery during the oil boom in the 1930s.

Dad and Mom's Wedding Day

Graduation took them to dad's first job with Continental Pipeline in Billings, Montana. Dad decided the pipeline business was not for him so he took a job with Kiewit Construction as an engineer in Omaha, Nebraska. Kiewit then transferred him to a job in Groveland, California, just west of Yosemite where he worked on a powerhouse job.

Mom was a city gal and used to the fineries of life while dad was more of a simple small-town guy. In the beautiful foothills of the Sierra Nevadas they lived in a small double wide trailer they had purchased with the help of a company loan and my mother's aunt. There were no neighbors except an old mare in a small coral and a big apple tree. The sound of logging trucks and compression brakes on the long winding roads were a daily event. The area did have some benefits though, as my dad purchased his first large caliber rifle, a Remington 30-06, to try his hand at deer hunting. There was a nice patch of woods directly behind the trailer that allowed my dad to find a spot on the many game trails and quietly wait for his chance at an unsuspecting buck. His first deer came on October 25th, 1965, at 6:15 p.m. It dressed out at eighty-five pounds. I was born on that October 1st.

My brother Scott came along a year later on December the 17th. Dad received a call one day from his Mom. The Army Corps of Engineers had sent him a letter and wanted to offer him a job in Anchorage. Much to my mom's naiveté at the time and my dad's enthusiasm to get back to Alaska, Mom acquiesced and agreed to the move, not knowing what she would be getting herself into.

Dad and Brian in the yard of our new trailer home

And so it was, north to Alaska, the land of the midnight sun and northern lights. The trailer was packed up and shipped up to Anchorage. Dad went ahead to prepare their new home while Mom went to visit relatives. By this time she was pregnant with my sister that would be due that spring. We arrived in Anchorage on December 23rd, 1967. The trailer my parents owned was, interestingly enough, the only trailer in the new park in Anchorage that had a brick chimney. I know this from many years later as we would drive by and see this, intrigued that my parents and my brother and I all once lived there. I was obviously too young to remember life in the double wide but found some solace in knowing a little about my roots and where I had come from. Dad soon bought a duplex in an area of town called Mountain View.

The duplex had some potential and Dad after all was an engineer, so plans were made to expand the unit over the garage area and make it into a triplex and to increase his cash flow from adding a second tenant. With the birth of child number three, my sister Carrie, the time was right for more space.

Our old duplex and Dad's new construction of a third apartment above the garages.

Anchorage had an interesting mixture of people, being a major military town. Amongst our neighbors was an Alaska Native couple that took a strong liking to Mom and Dad. They were quite well known in the area for their talent carving ivory and making beautiful grass baskets. One year they made each of us kids an authentic pair of native mukluks. These are boots worn by native children made from real sealskin and seal fur. The women actually chew the skin into shape and sew them by hand. Of course my mom would make us wear them much to our dislike as many of the kids in the area thought we were quite strange.

As time progressed Dad was offered a position with the federal government working as a civil engineer with the Federal Aviation Administration. He sold the triplex and had a new house built near a small lake and close to the University of Alaska.

It was at the FAA that Dad met men that would come to have a huge influence in his life and leave an impact that would change him forever.

Chapter 5
The Dream

"Keep close to Nature's heart...and break clear away, once in a while,
and climb a mountain or spend a week in the woods.
Wash your spirit clean."
-John Muir

Summers in Alaska are short and very intense. They typically last no more than three months. June through August is summertime. The sun is out much of the day and night and provides a long-anticipated break from the long winter months. Many Alaskans are highly outdoor-driven people. One has to be to truly enjoy the benefits that the beautiful country has to offer. It is during these months that fishing is at its peak and draws many out of the house and out into the river country.

Dad worked with a couple of guys at the FAA that were already very much involved in the finer side of Alaskan outdoor life. Lloyd Strid was a rugged man in his late 50s. He was what you would call a "jack of all trades" kind of fellow. Dad grew quite fond of spending time with Lloyd and I think looked up to him in almost a father figure way. Lloyd had boats and cabins and all kinds of "toys" to enjoy life in the great outdoors. Lloyd liked Dad too. He used to call him "Chuckers" as a fun term of affection and nickname of Chuck, which my dad normally went by.

It was Lloyd who turned my dad onto a great new program that the State was offering that would allow a resident to purchase property in specific designated areas at a very low price, with stipulations attached, of course. The program was the "open entry land program" offered by the state of Alaska's Division of Lands. It allowed individual residents to stake as much as 5 acres of land in certain state-selected areas. Lands available included blocks in the Susitna River valley north of Anchorage and near a town called Talkeetna. Under the program, my dad was able to choose 5 acres in any of these areas. The program allowed the individual to lease the land from the state for a filing fee of $10.00 and an annual lease fee of $40.00. I have a copy of the original lease receipt that was given to my dad dated April 15, 1971, from the State of Alaska, Department for Natural Resources, Division of Lands, for the sum of $50.00. It is incredible by today's standards to think that this was even possible.

Lloyd Strid had taken my dad to a remote town in the Susitna valley drainage by the name of Talkeetna. At the time Talkeetna had one small gas station, which also served as a grocery store, laundromat, and ice-cream parlor. Next to it stood the historic Talkeetna Roadhouse Inn. There was a tiny airstrip used by bush pilots and not too much else. Lloyd had constructed his own flat-bottom boat that held an outboard motor on the back. This served to get him up to a small piece of property where he had built a small log cabin. In 1970, the trip up the river would prove to be an all-day adventure many times, just getting to this very isolated location. It was up a major river, the Susitna, then up another major river, the Talkeetna, and then up another river called Clear Creek.

The going was slow and tedious and the small outboard would barely keep the boat on step and outpace the current of the river. It felt like moving in slow motion as you would watch the water flow by and look out towards the river bank, appearing to not even move. Little by little, though, progress was made against the mighty current. Each rapid created its own strategic difficulty. Shallow water is an extreme enemy to any outboard motor. Smashing into rocks and sucking up gravel and floating debris presented an ongoing problem for every trip. Many times it would be necessary to jump out of the boat and literally help pull it up through the shallow rapids. This was no easy feat as water was streaming by at a high velocity. Shallow or not, it made walking almost impossible. Wet feet were the norm as water regularly made its way over the tops of boots. This created a cold wet trip for the duration as the temperature on the river traveling upstream was always quite cool.

Arriving at the final destination was considered a victory itself. Exhausted, wet, and tired, and usually hungry was the norm.

Strid had built himself a cozy cabin set back off the creek 25 yards and surrounded by towering cottonwood trees, made the cabin out of small diameter spruce trees cut right off his property. The story goes that the cabin was built in a long weekend with a crew of friends and Strid's sons helping. This is an amazing fact when you realize what had to take place to allow this to come to fruition. Lloyd was a true craftsman and made his own furniture out of logs and wood. Inside the small cabin was a pot belly stove which when stoked would heat the cabin quite nicely even in the cold winter months. There were a set of bunk beds, all hand made and another couple of single beds next to the wall at the back of the one-room cabin. A small table with two chairs served as the dining area with a small wood counter in the corner as the kitchen area. The running water was the creek outside, the bathroom was the outhouse out back, and the light at night was from a Coleman propane lantern. A small fire pit sat out front of the porch with a handmade log bench and a tree stump cut out to form a high back chair.

Next to the cabin stood a 15-foot-high cache. A cache is a small log storage area that is put up on high stilt legs made of long narrow trees. Think of this as a mini log cabin on stilts. There was a tall wood ladder made of small diameter logs to the entry. Caches have long been a unique piece of Alaskan architecture and history. Pioneers stored their food supplies here to keep them out of the reach of the many types of animals that would love to get their paws on them.

The creek in front of the cabin was a very wide shallow rapid that ran diagonally across the creek to the other side. The shallows served as a very safe place for my brother and me to play when we were young and experimenting with our first pair of waders. The water was no more than 12 inches deep directly in front with many large rocks to help slow the current and enable us to safely wade for many yards out. It was particularly fun when the kings were running at the end of June and first few weeks of July. As they grew closer to spawning they would pair up in these protected shallow waters. Now when you are 8 years old and weigh 60 pounds, some of these salmon were as big as you. Nothing was more fun than to wade out and try to catch a king salmon. I am not talking about using a pole and line. I mean catching them by hand. That was the ultimate challenge. My brother Scott and I would spend hours out in the creek "catching" salmon. By this time in their life cycle they were extremely red in color and would stick out like a sore toe as my dad would say. You could simply spot your target and slowly work your way up from behind them so as to not be noticed. The only way to catch them was by the tail. We were successful many times and would proudly hold up our wriggling salmon, yelling up to the cabin for Dad to see.

Lloyd had introduced this great land to Dad and encouraged him to get his piece while he could.

For a long time Dad had the desire for owning his own getaway, a place to relax and call his own. This was it. Dad was set on getting land here and in this remote area of his newfound paradise.

Dad wanted to be as close as he could to Lloyd and was fortunate enough find, open and available, a beautiful piece of property that was just downstream from Strid's a few hundred yards. There was only one other piece of property between Dad and Strid. Each piece of property had several hundred feet of creek exposure. The property then went straight back in the form of a rectangle to a total size of approximately 5 acres.

And so the first step to his dream was fulfilled. With his land staked out, all that was needed was for him to then survey it and record it with the state. As fate would have it, Lloyd was also a registered surveyor. The state did not require this to be completed for a period of five years. Over the next few years, we were able to make the trip up to our property and stay at Strid's cabin while he was not using it.

Another close friend and colleague of Dad's that had also been a part of this adventure to build a cabin in the woods. Steve

Kurth had staked the property directly on the other side of the creek from Strid. Steve was able to actually start and build his cabin much sooner than Dad. By the end of the summer in 1975, Steve had his cabin completed. Steve was always very accommodating if we needed to use it when available as well.

Steve was married to Pat and father of four girls, all older than us except his youngest who was the same age as my youngest sister Tina. Steve was from Iowa where he was a farmer before making his way to Alaska with the Corp of Engineers in 1969, where he first met Dad. Dad later helped him get a job with the FAA.

Steve was a good friend of Dad's. They helped each other on building their boats, fixing motors, traveling to the property together and also hunted in the fall together. Steve was a very soft-spoken mild-mannered type unless he got roused by something and he could be as feisty as a wolverine. Not a large man in stature but I thought always very strong and hardworking. There was nothing he could not do. Like Lloyd, Steve was the do-it-yourself man. A perfect fit for anyone wanting to take on the remote lifestyle these men desired. As a young boy, I was always intrigued watching Steve roll his own cigarettes. He could carry a conversation with Dad and roll a perfect little stogie at the same time. I used to love the empty tobacco bags he would give me. I used them to keep "stuff" in them. I have many fond memories of spending time at his cabin and property before ours was built. Steve, Dad, and Lloyd had many adventures early in their first trips to the property. Steve used to run a canoe with an outboard motor all the way up the river and creek. He would literally have to buy a new prop for almost every trip until he could buy a motor with a jet.

Now that our land was staked, marked, and recorded, the next step was planning and building our cabin. It would not be until another five years that those plans would come to full fruition. Many trips were made to the property during those years. Dad had a large tent we would sometimes pitch on the spot he would ultimately choose to build. Other times we were able to use our friend's cabins. All the while, all of us were dreaming of the day we would soon have our own place.

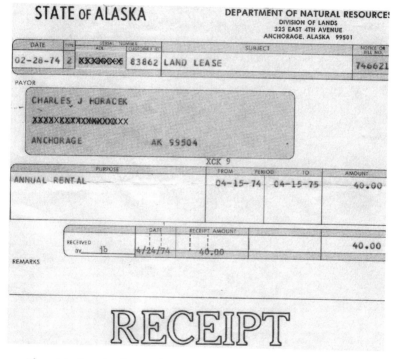

The original receipt that my dad had for the annual rental payment for his property to the State of Alaska. The date is 2-28-74, the amount $40.00. The lease period is shown here as 4-15-74 to 4-15-75.

CHARLES J. HORACEK	567
L. ADRIENNE HORACEK	
xxxxxxxxxxxxxxxxxxxxxxxxxx	
ANCHORAGE, ALASKA 99504	10/24 19 77 89-87 / 1252

PAY TO THE
ORDER OF _Alaska Dept of Revenue_ $ 66 21/

Sixty Six & 71/100 _____ DOLLARS

AlaskaPacificBank
BOX 420 / 601 W. 5th AVENUE
ANCHORAGE, ALASKA 99510

CHARTER CUSTOMER

Charles J Horacek

MEMO _PDL_ xxxxxxxxx

The original check written to pay the State of Alaska the balance my dad owed to purchase the property that he had originally been leasing. The $40.00 yearly lease was credited toward the final price of $100.00. (with a small fee added)

Dad was always very proud to share this as we would be sitting around the campfire after a long day fishing and someone would inevitably ask him, "So Chuck, what did you pay for this place?"

Dad would always get a good chuckle at the look on their face when he told them.

Brian Horacek

77- 0 0 2 3 1 1

WP48 5-

RECORDED-FILED
TALKEETNA REC.
DISTRICT

'77 DEC 5 PM 2 38

MAT-SU TITLE INSURANCE AGENCY INC
WASILLA AIRPORT MALL
P.O. BOX 1810
WASILLA, ALASKA 99687

State of Alaska

Patent

BOOK **65** PAGE **692**
Talkeetna Recording District

6o4l2   No. 3503

Know All Men By These Presents that the State of Alaska in consideration of the sum of
ONE HUNDRED AND NO/100--- DOLLARS,
lawful money of the United States and other good and valuable consideration, now paid, the receipt
whereof is hereby acknowledged, does hereby grant to ....

.... CHARLES J. HORACEK

.... XXXXXXXXXXXXXXXX Anchorage, Alaska 99504

.... his .... heirs and assigns all the real property situated in the Borough of Matanuska-Susitna ,
State of Alaska, described as follows:

> ALASKA STATE LAND SURVEY 74-134, LOCATED
> WITHIN SECTION 33, TOWNSHIP 27 NORTH, RANGE 4
> WEST, SEWARD MERIDIAN, CONTAINING 4.84 ACRES, MORE
> OR LESS, ACCORDING TO THE SURVEY PLAT RECORDED
> IN THE TALKEETNA RECORDING OFFICE ON JUNE 15, 1977
> AS PLAT NO. 77-42.
>
> Subject to platted easements.

Township ... 27 NORTH ... Range ... 4 WEST ... SEWARD ... Meridian,
Alaska, according to the official survey thereof save and except those restrictions appearing in the Federal Patent or
other conveyance by which the Grantor acquired title and further, Alaska, the Grantor, expressly reserves, out of
the grant hereby made, unto itself, its lessees, successors, and assigns forever, all oils, gases, coal, ores, minerals,
fissionable materials, and fossils of every name, kind or description, and which may be in or upon said lands above
described, or any part thereof, and the right to explore the same for such oils, gases, coal, ores, minerals,fissionable
materials and fossils, and it also hereby expressly saves and reserves out of the grant hereby made, unto itself, its
lessees, successors and assigns forever, the right to enter by itself, its or their agents, attorneys, and servants upon
said lands, or any part or parts thereof, at any and all times, for the purpose of opening, developing, drilling and
working mines or wells on these or other lands, and taking out and removing therefrom all such oils, gases, coal,
ores, minerals, fissionable materials and fossils, and to that end it further expressly reserves out of the grant hereby
made, unto itself, its lessees, successors, and assigns forever, the right by its or their agents, servants and attorneys
at any and all times to erect, construct, maintain, and use all such buildings, machinery, roads, pipelines, power-
lines, and railroads, sink such shafts, drill such wells, remove such soil, and to remain on said lands or any part
thereof for the foregoing purposes and to occupy as much of said lands as may be necessary or convenient for such
purposes hereby expressly reserving to itself, its lessees, successors, and assigns, as aforesaid, generally all rights
and power in, to, and over said land, whether herein expressed or not, reasonably necessary or convenient to render
beneficial and efficient the complete enjoyment of the property and rights hereby expressly reserved.

To Have and to Hold the said land with the appurtenances thereof unto the said Grantee and
.. his .. heirs and assigns forever.

*The original patent the State of Alaska issued my dad for the survey and
purchase of the land*

47

Chapter 6
The Boats

"Courage, hard work, self-mastery, and
intelligent effort are all essential to a successful life."
-Theodore Roosevelt

The rivers in Alaska are some of the most difficult in the world to navigate. Most are fast moving water with rocky bottoms that create shallow rock bars that can prove almost impassable. An outboard motor with a propeller is simply not a viable option. The prop needs to be low in the water to provide the necessary power to propel the boat upstream against the heavy current. This in turn leads to major prop damage from the rocks. A flat bottom boat with a jet is the best way to go, although some have opted for air boats or large-hulled jet boats. This is fine if you don't mind being cursed every time you pass by another boat or fisherman on the shore.

Dad and his friends were some of the first to navigate up the Talkeetna River and Clear Creek by boat. I think what made my dad unique was that for many years he never bought a boat, he made his own. This was accomplished by designing a flat bottom boat that would be light enough to not draw too much water and that could carry the loads required. These river boats, known as jet sleds in the lower 48 states, proved to be the most efficient at the time.

Dad built his first boat in 1972. It was a plywood boat with a flat bottom and raised bow and reinforced transom that would be able to handle an outboard motor with a jet unit. Dad got his inspiration and ideas from his good friend and mentor Lloyd Strid who already had a viable prototype and boat he used to access his cabin on Clear Creek.

The boat would be completely constructed of wood. The bottom and sides would be made of half inch plywood with ribs made from standard 2x4s. Dad devoted half of our two car garage to his boat building area. He laid out and cut all the wood and assembled his boat with screws and a marine epoxy for extra strength. Wood that needed to be bent would be soaked in water and then steamed with Mom's iron. The process was slow and tedious. The boat was approximately 24 feet long and 4 feet wide, slightly narrower at the bow and stern. It had two large wood bench seats built in for seating and extra strength. Once the wood frame was constructed he used a fiberglass epoxy coating for the seams and bottom and painted the whole boat with an epoxy marine paint. Meanwhile the neighbors would stop by from time to time to see what Chuck was doing in his garage. I'm sure many wondered if the thing would even float much less transport our family up a river.

One of dad's boats being built in our garage.

Dad was so excited to use his boat that the first summer it was ready he didn't even wait for the paint job to be completed before getting it out on the water. Many of the early photos I have of him are in his mostly completed boat still showing the wood without paint. It proved to be a good boat and would do the job of getting us up the river and to the property where we would soon have our cabin.

Dad bought a Mercury 50-h.p. outboard motor with a short shaft and tiller handle. He later mounted it on a homemade metal and wood lift to enable him to raise the motor up or down based on the water depth and circumstances. Usually this

Dad, Scott, Carrie and Brian fishing in 1972

meant that rather than bumping rocks and damaging the lower unit he could push a long handle that would lift the motor up. It was helpful when varying weight loads would cause the boat to perform differently. Dad could make a slight adjustment in the motor height and that would allow the motor to perform at an optimal level.

Dad soon discovered that owning a boat and motor meant also learning how to fix a boat and motor. The river was nothing short of punishing on both boat and motor. It was not uncommon for the motor to have problems of one sort or another during a trip up the river. This might not seem like such a big deal but if you are miles away from any town or potential help it sure put things into perspective quickly. We spent many hours on the gravel bars that line the river while dad stood leg deep in the water trying to trouble shoot his motor problems. Sometimes it was a water pump, other times a shear pin. He learned how to fix his own motors on the spot. He had no real choice, of course, as his family was usually sitting there in the boat or scouring the rock bar for treasures as my brother and I liked to do.

To drop a lower shaft from an outboard motor that is mounted on the back of a boat on the side of a river is an art form to itself. The water is near freezing cold. You would have to not only get your arms wet but have to also be agile enough to operate a wrench while holding a freezing cold piece of metal in the other hand. Simultaneously he had to make sure not to drop the bolts or nuts into the rushing river. Dad learned over the years what types of spare parts he needed to carry to be equipped for all these possible maintenance issues. He also spent many hours at home in his shop rebuilding and overhauling his motors. He had manuals and help from some of his friends at times but for the most part learned as he went along.

Shallow water was his main nemesis. If it was too shallow then the motor's jet unit would suck up small rocks or hit large rocks damaging the unit. Each time a rock is struck the boat would momentarily loose power as the jet would rise into the air and then suck air into the intake instead of water. What a sound this would make. The combination of fast moving metal striking a solid rock could shock life back into the dead. This was a dreaded sound if you were a passenger hoping to get to your favorite fishing place more quickly than not. Sometimes the boat won the battle and others the river. There were many times we had to bail out of the side of the boat to pull it upstream through the shallows. Not an easy task when walking on slippery rocks in 2-3 feet of water. It is impossible to regain power and momentum to go up the shallows once the boat has slowed to a low speed and looses buoyancy and the advantage of being on the step.

There were many times traveling the river we had motor problems in precarious places. It never failed to occur at the most un-opportune times.

This is one reason we always kept an anchor tied to a rope and the front of the boat. There were times we did not have the ability to land the boat on the river bank and would have to use oars, get out of the boat and pull, or as a last resort throw the anchor line and hoped it caught.

There was one memorable experience that happened with Dad and Chris. They were traveling down river when the motor went out.

There happened to be a dangerous part of the river just downstream and since they were close to the bank of the river, Chris threw the anchor line. It caught and held but caused the boat to swing hard with a fast jolt that Chris had not anticipated. He was thrown off the boat and into the freezing water. Dad was quick to react the only way a father would if he saw his son floating down the river, He jumped in after him. Dad reached Chris and they floated down the river together until they were able to reach a tree and stop their momentum and get out of the water. Wet and cold, they sat for a passer-by in another boat. Fortunately they didn't have to wait too long. Sometimes things happen and you have to make the best of it. Chris will tell you that his dad clearly saved his life that day and was a hero to all of us.

Dad built a total of three boats over the course of about 12 years. The long wood boats had the capacity and ability to go where heavier aluminum boats could not. There were also disadvantages to the wood boats with the biggest being the short life span of the boat due to the rugged water and rocks. One main advantage of the wood was the ability to repair a leak. All that was needed was some spare wood and epoxy and we were back in business.

Dad then took a great interest in rubber boats similar to what the Coast Guard uses on the sea. They proved to be extremely buoyant and light weight and able to handle the swift water and rocks due to enhanced technology in the thickness and type of rubber. After much research and discussion he made the move to purchase his first boat.

Dad's Zodiac with Chris

The days of the old wood boat that had so faithfully carried us up the river were soon put behind for a more lighter and maneuverable craft. Far less power was needed to propel our new Zodiac. It was easier for Dad to see the upcoming changes in the water and to maneuver around rocks and trees. The main drawback to the craft was its size. We could not fit nearly the load in our new boat that we had been able to carry with the larger, longer wood boats. This created a problem of having to make multiple trips up and down the river.

This is a photo of Dad's friend Steve Kurth in his Zodiac

Many might think that a rubber boat could not handle the harshness of rocks and trees in the water. I was amazed at the strength and integrity that the Zodiac provided and we soon grew fond of our new mode of river transportation. Dad operated the Zodiac for several years before deciding that he had enough and needed something better. Not sure what the perfect solution was he then turned to aluminum.

Our first aluminum jet sled creek-side in front of the cabin

The aluminum sled was light and easy to operate. It had more capacity than his Zodiac yet not as much as the larger wood boats had in years past.

It seemed sufficient and had less maintenance involved than wood. The main problem did not develop until after a few years when it became apparent that the riveted aluminum was too susceptible to leakage. The boat just could not take the constant pounding it would endure on the water and rocks of the river.

The jet sled in action

Dad finally decided to take the big plunge of spending the money needed to get a larger, more structurally sound welded aluminum boat that would also provide some shelter from the elements while traveling the river. This was a long awaited and welcomed change to my mom. The boat included an electric bilge, lights, power lift and fuel and oil injection. It drove like a dream. It too had a major disadvantage, which was it could not navigate the truly shallow waters of Clear Creek. It was only useable if the water in the creek was high enough to allow it to perform to its peak ability. Shallow water was left to the older smaller lighter aluminum boat. Thus began the era of using two boats rather than one.

Dad's new boat

I had the opportunity to pilot both over the years and certainly liked the power and ability of the larger welded aluminum boat but knew that it had its time and place and limitations when it came to running shallow water. Dad was so proud of his new boat. He had never spent a lot of money on a boat while I was growing up and I was happy to see him finally have something really nice. It is unfortunate that he would only have a few years use of it before he passed away in 2005.

Chapter 7
Cabin Crew

"No matter what your lot in life may be,
build something on it"
-Unknown

Early in the spring of 1976 we began the preparation for building our family cabin. The first task was identifying enough suitable trees to use in construction. This would be a true Alaskan log cabin built with logs from the native trees on our property. The most common pine tree was the Alaskan black spruce *Piciea mariana*. The tree grew fairly well in the moist fertile soil of the lower areas near the river. Each tree would need to be identified, measured, cut, trimmed, stripped, cured, cut again, notched, and finally placed in position. No small task.

In the spring, the grass is still low, the alder trees have not grown their leaves and much of the brush is also less dense than in the summer. This makes locating and getting to the trees easier. This is also the time of year many of the animals are starting to be more active. Black bears and grizzly bears are very common in this part of Alaska. Dad was always very cognizant of this fact and always carried a loaded sawed-off 12-gauge shotgun with bear slugs loaded and ready to be used. Bear encounters are a mom's worst fear with young children out in the woods. There is more on this subject in Chapter 13.

Dad would always be mindful of where we were and what we were doing while we were young and not carrying a weapon for protection.

The only bad thing about building a log cabin is the main essential element, trees. "They don't move themselves," Dad would always say when we were tired and didn't want to work. I loved fishing from a young age and was always easily lured to the creek to throw a line in. There was not to be much fishing for the next few years. Work was the reason to be there if we were to have the cabin we always wanted. Dad became a master of the chainsaw, like most other tools. Our whole cabin was in the hands of the chainsaw. In fact we needed two. One larger 18-inch Homelite was used for cutting and also had a very handy winch attachment that would prove to be worth its weight in gold. The smaller was used to trim branches and form the notches for constructing the cabin.

Dad would run the chainsaw and begin the cut; each tree would need to be felled in the proper direction, towards the designated cabin site to allow for easier transporting. Once the lower cut was made straight through the tree about three-quarters of the diameter, he would then begin the angled second cut to form the notch to direct the fall. Once complete, the section that was cut was knocked out with a large hatchet leaving a gap.

After making sure we were all clear, the final cut was made at the backside, which would then allow the tree to break free from the original trunk and fall to the ground. This of course was the exciting part for my brother and me who would always make sure to yell the proverbial "TIMBER." The tree would come crashing down with a thunder and the cracking of breaking branches.

Next was the trimming of the tree. All branches have to be completely cut off. Once free from the tree, they have to be discarded to the side out of the way. Smaller branches can be cut with a machete or small axe or a small chainsaw. Once this task was completed the tree would then need to be prepared to be moved to the building site.

A small winch on the chainsaw was our main source of power. The chainsaw was anchored to a large tree usually about a hundred feet or so away from the tree that had been cut. The blade was removed and replaced with the winch. A long rope was attached to the winch and the tree to be moved. One of us boys was responsible for operating the chainsaw winch while the other helped Dad with directing the cut tree. The winch would have to slowly begin pulling the rope to take out all the slack and then once slack was out the fallen tree would jump forward a few feet. Then the process was repeated until the tree was moved close enough to the winch to require moving to another anchor tree. The tree had to be winched butt first. This is the larger end. The reason is the tip of the tree was too small a diameter usually to be effective. In order to allow the winch to do its work with pulling, the butt end of the tree would have to be up off the ground enough to move forward. This was accomplished by providing a smaller diameter tree placed horizontally to the tree being pulled, allowing it to roll on the smaller tree. The butt end would also need to be lifted at the exact time the rope was taut and ready to pull, enabling it to jump forward without digging into the soft ground. This didn't always go as planned. When the butt would get stuck, we would have to dig out in front of it, allowing it to move forward on the next pull.

This is not done without danger. One would have to make sure to never be directly in front to the tree while it was being pulled. The easiest position to accomplish this was straddling the log while lifting or using a smaller log as a lever to help lift and jump the tree forward.

Once at the building site the logs were stacked. It was then necessary to strip the bark off the tree. The machete was again the tool of choice. With trial and error we found how to scrape large strips off while the tree was still green. If the logs were left to dry before being stripped, the bark was much harder to remove in large strips. Once the log was stripped it would need to be rolled to get the bottom side. The log was then ready to sit and cure. All of our logs were left to dry at least a year before using.

This process was repeated, weekend after weekend for the entire summer until enough logs were staged for construction.

The beginning of the cabin construction, Mike Kurth in the hat next to Dad with his son James on the left, Scott is next to Dad shooting his BB gun.

The cabin would be anchored to four treated posts, like those used for telephone poles. These posts were made of treated timber and brought up the river in the boat one at a time. Each post was about 18" in diameter and approximately 8 feet long. To place them in the ground we had to dig large holes. We then back-filled them with river rocks and soil. This is not an easy proposition in a land that has permafrost about 12 inches below the surface. Permafrost is just as it sounds, ground that is permanently frozen. The ground would have to be "chipped" through. Once the permafrost was penetrated, the ground was relatively easy to dig. The main logs that are laid on the posts were notched to fit on top and then secured with a large spike. Once the first level of logs is laid, the rest is easy.

The "crew," Dad on the left, Scott behind him, Lloyd Strid, Steve Kurth, and Mike Kurth.

Dad cutting a notch in a log

The walls are almost complete

The floor joists are 4x4s cut into the logs

Rough-cut of the door opening

Rafters are now in and supported by the ends of the cabin. These are larger diameter logs to provide support for the heavy sod roof and to bear the load of the snow in the winter months.

Cabin walls are completed

Dad with Lloyd Strid, Gene Strid and his wife and son

All the logs have been laid, the door cut out, and the roof put on. This is how the cabin looked after the completion of the first full summer of construction, 1977

Chapter 8
Cabin Life

"The mark of a successful man is one that has spent an entire day on the bank of a river without feeling guilty about it."
-Unknown

Dad's favorite spot was sitting on a bench in his "front yard" overlooking the creek.

Our cabin was the perfect escape from the busy life of living in the city. It was never built with the intention of us living in it for a long period of time. My dad worked hard as a civil engineer during the week and when Friday came he was ready for a change of pace and scenery. If anyone has ever tried to take their family camping for a weekend, I think it is safe to say that it is certainly not easy. The amount of preparation and planning is a couple of nights work by itself. Dad was always willing to pay this price for the opportunity to enjoy what he had built. His desire outweighed the pain involved in orchestrating the weekly summer routine of going to the cabin.

For most this might involve driving the necessary two and a half hours to a favorite camping spot. Not my dad. This was not far enough away from people and civilization to suit his needs. He had to build a cabin where it required a challenging river boat trip on top of the two and a half hour drive to get to our family cabin. This was not a passion that was his own. He was fortunate enough to have friends who shared the same passion and often traveled at the same time.

This book will refer to our numerous weekend trips over the many summers, 35 to be exact. There was a time when we felt as though we spent as much time there as we did at our own home in Anchorage. Much of this time was to my mom's chagrin as she was often left at home with my younger siblings to care for. Dad was good at escaping some of those duties. This was a trait that I too learned well and have been known to practice on occasion.

Weekends at the cabin were often a way for my dad to spend time developing some of those important fatherly bonds a dad needs to develop with his children. Much time was spent learning and practicing many of the things one needs to learn about the outdoors. Dad was always a patient teacher and afforded us kids much grace with trying new things not to mention his patience.

There were always plenty of things to do at the cabin. It was a veritable project playground and a never-ending job. Although

Brian Horacek

the cabin was completed, it really never was. Dad would always find something to do to improve it or make it better. When the cabin was finished it was then time to build a sauna. My dad always had an agenda in mind each trip to the cabin. Sometimes he would choose to share that with us and other times we never really knew until we got there. That usually meant there was work for us to do and he just didn't want to tell us about it until we were actually there and unable to escape it. That is if we wanted to eat. A dad always has leverage he can use when he needs to. "Work before play" was one of his mottos. "How can you justify spending time fishing if there was firewood that needed to be cut."

Many of our trips where centered round just plain leisure time. What is the point if you are going to have a place like this and not enjoy it? This was the part I liked. Leisure at the cabin means fishing. When the salmon are running, there is a freezer to fill. That becomes the project. It was a good thing we had plenty of fish in the river. The work actually begins after the fish are caught. Once the cooler was full for the weekend, we were then free to do other things kids like to do.

While we were young, my brother and I loved to play around the cabin and creek. We were careful to never get too far away but always far enough to feel independent from our dad. Often this involved walking up the trail to our neighbor's cabin or down the creek to a favorite fishing spot on the beavers' dam. I think we both liked helping Dad the most, whatever he was doing. There were not many times I saw my dad sit idly and do nothing.

A cabin in the woods in Alaska takes work to keep it up. It is that simple. If you want to enjoy what the outdoors offers, you have to pay the price. Early spring was a time to cut fallen trees from the previous winter for firewood. Dad would usually find one not too far from the cabin and we would take turns operating the chain saw to cut the limbs off and then cut the tree into the appropriately sized sections to make firewood. Once cut, the sections would need to be carried back to the woodpile at the cabin. They were then stacked and covered to dry and cure in order to be able to split them when the time came. This was of course a never ending project. We enjoyed having a campfire while spending time at the cabin. It was just a part of the ritual. Late afternoon we would start the fire, not because we needed the heat but because it added to the experience and we just plain enjoyed it. A campfire helps to keep the voracious Alaskan mosquitoes at bay and also provides the main means of cooking our dinner.

As we grew older, my siblings and I learned to enjoy this time together sharing a drink and talking about life and telling stories. We would spend hours around the campfire, enjoying the time and the beautiful scenery around us. It seemed to take a decade or two before Dad finally decided to erect a crude covering for the campfire pit area. We used some smaller-sized saplings about 4 inches in diameter at the base and about ten feet high. These provided the main supports. We then attached small 1x1s at an angle joining the main beam which was the higher pole. Over this structure we secured a large tarp that was then fastened to the frame with a nylon cord through the grommets. This worked well when it was raining out and we didn't have to miss our campfire just due to inclement weather conditions. The tarp was left up for the duration of the summer, occasionally needing to be straightened or tightened. It was high enough to avoid the fire flames and suited my dad just fine. Why it took so long for this addition is beyond me. I guess it was always just a matter of taking the time and there was always so much to do that it was a lower priority.

When spring strikes, it comes with a vengeance. The summers in Alaska are quite short compared with the lower 48 states. We would leave the cabin with a dull grey tone to everything only to return to a newly greened dash of vegetation, then to a jungle-like look. The small shrubs and grasses grow extremely fast due to the longer summer days. There would be 6 inch tall grass in areas where nothing was showing the previous week. The modern-day gas-operated weed eater was a gift made for this specific situation. This was a welcomed replacement for the old machete hanging behind the cabin door. This was a job usually Dad chose to tackle on his own. He was a one-man grass-cutting machine with his new weed eater.

See the color photos in the middle of the book for a view of the cabin before and after trimming the grass and shrubs.

The area that was once dense with shrubs and grasses behind and to the sides of the cabin became a newly cut field or rough lawn. Dad was never concerned with the aesthetic appeal as much as he was with the general safety of the area. The shorter the surrounding ground cover, the sooner you could see approaching bears. This was the prime concern always with his children. It did tend to add to the appearance and help make the land look kept. Small alder trees became fuel for the smoker. Large Devils Clubs were removed to help reduce the random occurrence of stepping on one or brushing up against it while walking. For those that haven't had the pleasure of experiencing a Devil's Club, it is a small shrub with large thorns or spines that protrude out of the stem. Devil's Club (*Oplopanax horridus,*) is a native plant found along the costal areas of the Pacific Northwest and Alaska. It will penetrate most clothing and leaves a very sore irritated incursion point on the skin. Not a fun thing to run into.

The creek water level is always high in the spring and tends to drop as the snowmelt in the mountains comes to an end. The shallower water brings work to be done on the creek bank in front of the cabin. Fifteen years or so ago, I built a rock dam on the edge of the creek bank to serve as a protected mooring for the boat. This was a project that took several summers to get to the right size and proportion to actually work. It is more of a river rock jetty of sorts. The jetty, or rock dam, is strong enough for people to stand on and redirects the current of the main channel as it flows along our side of the creek. It is amazing to see how it has fared over the years. It provides a natural hole below it that serves as a great spot for salmon to lay out of the strong current on their way to their spawning grounds. It also serves as a great place to fish, wash your hands, pots and pans, and just stand and watch the fish swim by. The high water inevitably washes some of the rocks out of position each year, requiring someone to move them back. This is a perfect chore on a hot summer day. The cold water is a refreshing way to cool off while lifting and pitching rocks that weigh from 50 to 100 pounds each. The water provides an amazing amount of buoyancy for moving large rocks. Without the water helping, this would be an unbearable chore. The satisfaction of building something that can actually withstand the power the river is an amazing experience. Over the many years many people have helped keep it maintained and intact.

See color photos in the middle of the book for a view of the rock jetty.

The cabin is in an area that has no utilities. This means there is no power, telephone, or water service. Imagine that, out in the woods without electricity. The habit of walking in the front door and flicking a switch is far removed. Our lighting is from nature most of the time. When it does get dark enough to actually need a light, we have propane lights in the cabin. Small wall-mounted lanterns serve the purpose just fine. It is always a good idea to keep a flashlight handy at night once the lights do go out for the anticipated trip to the privy (outhouse).

Heat is a luxury. When the weather is not optimal and colder than normal, a nice warm fire is lit in the small barrel stove in the center of the cabin. I can not remember the last time it was lit during the summer. Winter is a different story. What is a luxury then becomes an essential.

A four-burner propane stove rests in the counter top on the right side of the cabin. This serves as the main area for cooking. All the essentials of any rural kitchen can be found in and around the kitchen cabinet area. Many staples are kept secure and stored here during the summer months and many through the winter too. Dad is usually the first one up in the mornings and can be heard filling the old percolator pot with water and making coffee. The sound of the large plank front door creaks open as he makes his way out to his favorite seat to start the day. Often he would be back in the cabin making breakfast before any of us had crawled out of our sleeping bags. The sound of bacon sizzling on the griddle and its aroma filling the air in the cabin is one of my favorite things.

Mom and Carrie in the kitchen area of the cabin

Meals are mostly served outside the cabin either around the fire pit or at the picnic table in the front of the cabin.

Mealtime

Dirty dishes at the cabin are one of my least favorite things. The lack of a conventional dishwasher is another luxury my generation has never experienced. Dish water is simply heated in a large pot on the stove; a small plastic tub is filled with hot water and serves as the sink to wash. Another tub is filled with rinse water. Several years ago Dad brought an old sink up to the cabin along with the old counter top and mounted it on the front porch to help serve the same purpose as it would at home for holding water to wash dishes. A jug of water is mounted above with a soap holder to offer a convenient place to wash hands. I prefer to use the creek myself. Sand is a great natural way to scrub pots and the never-ending supply of fresh water flowing by, a great way to rinse them.

Bathing is usually not needed for a short weekend trip. The creek provides plenty of fresh water to clean up and wash your hair if you choose. A sauna is an excellent way to get some of that salmon smell off and sweat out any remaining unwanted toxins from the previous night. A heated tin tub rests atop the rocks on the

The old barrel stove in the center of the cabin. Bunk beds can be seen behind it along the back wall

sauna stove providing an excellent way to wash up. The front porch of the sauna is screened slightly from the cabin allowing for soaping and rinsing and shampooing one's hair. A few minutes out in the cool air helps dry the body and is a very refreshing experience.

See the color photos in the middle of the book.

A typical privy or outhouse is just a short walk from the cabin to the downstream side. This provides all the normal comforts of home. My mom over the years has added her decorating touch by making sure that it is painted and filled with sunflower motif. A few magazines are neatly

Ladder to the front loft sleeping area

stacked and a padded seat provides a nice view to the south with the door open. The paper is stored in empty coffee cans to keep the squirrels from creating a mess. I don't know that there is a finer outhouse in the woods than ours.

See the color photos in the middle of the book.

A hammock lies between two large trees next to the cabin and is a favorite napping spot for many. It is large enough for two people to lie next to each other and has provided some fun times for the kids.

Carrie and me relaxing in the hammock

Cabin life includes dealing with the many different pests and creatures that live in the surrounding area. One of the most predominant is our local squirrels. During the cold winter months squirrels tend to seek shelter where ever they can find it. Often this tends to be the cabin. They are very crafty little creatures and have the ability to find a hole or make a hole to get where they want. On one memorable occasion, we returned from the previous summer to find that a squirrel had taken up residence in the cabin. He had built a nice nest on one of the sleeping bags in the loft. He proceeded to pack enough food to live a lifetime. What a mess to clean. No matter what you do it is impossible to keep them out of the cabin during the winter months. They know how to get in and out at their will.

A Spruce Beetle. They look more intimidating than what they actually are.
(Photo by Jim Rogers)

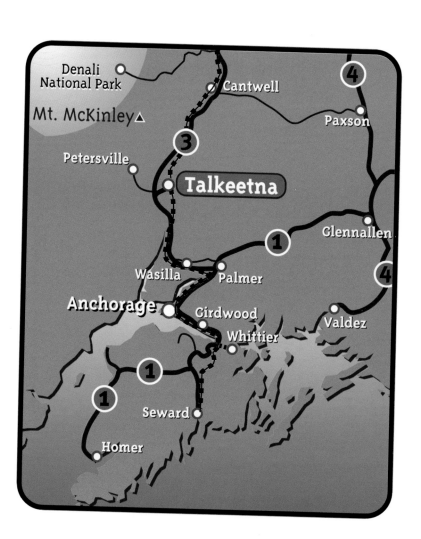

Mt. McKinley from outside Talkeetna

Horacek cabin original site ~ 1980

Clear Creek upstream view from cabin

Log sauna with original sod roof

Clear Creek record shallow water in 2004

Three bald eagles in tree next to the cabin

Fishing with Dad ~ 1972

Dad's first boat unpainted ~ 1972

Rockbar along Clear Creek upstream from cabin

Black bear in a tall Cottonwood tree next to cabin

Dad cooking breakfast for the family ~ 1972

Dad with a nice king salmon ~ 1971

Grizzly bear across the creek from the cabin

Outhouse made from old siding

Outhouse after Mom's decorating job

Two cow moose, very close!

Dad with Hank after a successful fishing trip

Boat full of live Silver Salmon on a stringer

Brian with a large King Salmon

Horacek cabin ~ 1987

Dad with Perry & Frank, dad's largest wood boat

Hank and Dad with a large King Salmon

Jim and Hank canning salmon steaks to take home

Dad holding a nice Sockeye (Red)
Salmon

Small grizzly on the creek

John Horacek with a large dog salmon

Dad's pride and joy

Dad and Hank enjoying a nice fishing hole

Captain Scott Horacek

Mom, digging steps up from the creek

Horacek cabin ~ 2004

Winter looking downstream, Photo – Scott Horacek

Cabin in winter of 2007, Photo – Scott Horacek

Winter view upstream, Photo – Scott Horacek

Cabin after 1986 flood

09/01/2006

Cabin after 2006 flood

Brian fishing off rock jetty in front of cabin

Chris Horacek fishing

Brian with a nice Rainbow

Hank with a beautiful bow

View of the Alaska Range and the Talkeetna River

Dad and Talia Horacek with bullet shells on fingers

Carrie and Jaeden Horacek

Carrie smoking salmon

Kim, Jaeden, and Talia with a nice sockeye salmon

Jaeden enjoying a sunny day fishing

Dad and Hank enjoying lunch in the cabin

Kim and Talia brave the wind traveling upstream

Dr. Jeff Horacek with a nice Silver Salmon

Clear Creek upstream on a grey day

Dad and Jim Marshall

"Happy Hank"

Small grizzly on the creek

Chapter 9
High Waters I

"Life is 10 percent what happens to you and
90 percent how you react to it"
-Charles Swindoll

During the fall of 1986 there was an excessive amount of rainfall in the mountains that feed the drainage areas into Clear Creek. Heavy rain is normal this time of year but this year it would prove to be more than the land could absorb. Normal heavy rain usually brings with it high dirty water. The once clear and clean water turns to a murky gray color. The force of the water usually will take out trees that are close to the bank that has been eroding over the years and carry them downstream. The water is littered with debris from branches and trees. As the water rises it washes out the bank on the side of the creek where the channel flows. As a precaution and safety measure we have on occasion cut a large tree that is close to the bank and potentially ready to fall and be swept away.

Scott cutting a large tree to protect the bank from erosion

Before cutting the tree we would fasten a large diameter steel cable around the butt of the tree and above the cut. When the tree is felled, it is swept up along the side of the bank and is now able to act as a barrier to the rushing high water and help with controlling erosion.

It is not uncommon for the creek to rise several feet very quickly with rain. When the rain subsides the creek slowly returns to normal. In 1986 this did not happen. The rain came and did not stop for days. According to the Old Farmers Almanac, on October 9 there were clear skies and there was no rain. The next day, it rained 2.56 inches in Talkeetna. The following day, October 10, it rained 5.16 inches and the rain did not stop until October17. The rainfall levels in the mountains are usually much higher than the levels recorded in town. The creek rose to a level that we had not ever seen. It was clearly not your normal flood. This type of flood is said to come once every 50 to 100 years. The effects from a flood like this can be devastating to anything in its path. The water rose to 12 feet above its normal level. The effects are almost impossible to explain other than to say where you see the cabin in the following photos; it is literally hanging over the bank of the creek. To tell you that we had over 50 feet of land in front of our cabin that we had to walk up a path to get up to the cabin is unimaginable.

During this time I was away at college and my dad took these photos from the air and later during a subsequent trip up to the cabin to assess the damage. We were sure that we were going to loose our treasured family cabin in this flood. My dad sent me a short letter while I was away at school with these photos. They show the devastation and the monumental task of trying to save the cabin.

Dad is an engineer by trade and so are all of his friends. Together these men rallied behind our family and pitched in their time, energy, and effort to find a solution. With some ingenuity and hard work they managed to devise a plan to elevate the cabin with winches. Once lifted from the foundation, they rigged a pulley system to pull the cabin back on logs to the new site. All the photos you see were taken during this process and show the complexity of this task.

If it had not been for the help from Steve Kurth, Mike Kurth, and Dan Pavey, our fellow Clear Creek neighbors, we would have not been able to save our cabin from certain destruction. We are forever grateful to all who helped in that process.

Today you would never know that the cabin was not built where it presently sits. You would also never be able to tell how much land we actually lost in front of the cabin from the floodwaters.

Everything was restored back to normal and has been that way since the flood.

Aerial photo of the flood waters

Mouth of Clear Creek where it joins the Talkeetna River. This is at flood stage and three times normal size. There is usually no water in the upper half of the photo.

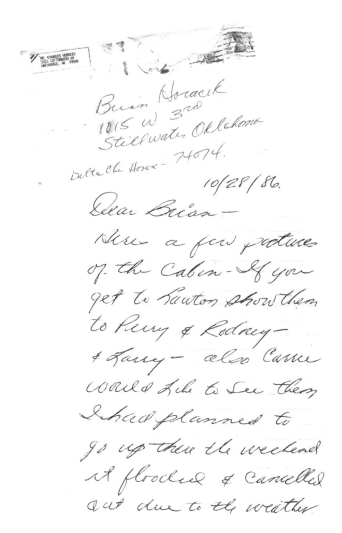

Dear Brian-
Here a few photos of the cabin- If you get to Lawton show them to Perry & Rodney & Larry- also Carrie would like to see them. I had planned to go up there the weekend it flooded & cancelled out due to the weather.

Glad I didn't, as I probably would have gone out to take a leak
at 2 a.m. and fell off the porch into the river- Ha
You can't imagine the damage- and the hundreds of trees that
are scattered all over the river.

– 2 –

*well – I just wanted
to send these pictures
to you – So you could
see what happened at
the cabin – It will
probably take a couple
of summers to restore
back what we had –
a new foundation under
the cabin – rebuild the
front porch – a new fire
Pit area and Benches*

Well I just wanted to send these pictures to you so you could see what happened at the cabin – It will probably take a couple of summers to restore back what we had- a new foundation under the cabin-rebuild the front porch- a new fire pit area and benches relocate the out house back- not to mention the damage to the cabin while we were moving it- But we'll get it done-

Well, keep your nose to the grindstone and your chin up- See you at Xmas.
~ Love Dad

The front porch of the cabin is hanging over the bank

Dad ~
10/17/86
From the water to the porch it's about 8 ft – the water was
about 12 feet above normal for this time of year

View of the cabin from downstream. The water has receded several feet now.

Dad ~ 10/86
The tree leaning over is the one that had the hammock on it, closest to the path to the outhouse. You can see part of the rope hanging on the tree.

Cabin roped and winched back on logs

Dad ~

Moving the cabin – using two winches, jacks, and come-a-longs- it's a lot of work.

The area that the cabin was sitting before the flood soon became the new front lawn and an open area for us to put a picnic table. The fire pit that was once on the down-stream side of the front of the cabin was washed away by the flood and had to be replaced on the upstream side of the cabin. Many of these changes are hard to imagine if we did not have the photos.

Chapter 10
Hilltop Hank's Place

"The person who tries to live alone will not succeed as a human being. His heart withers if it does not answer another heart. His mind shrinks away if he hears only the echoes of his own thoughts and finds no other inspiration."
-Pearl S Buck

There was a strange encounter during the summer of 1985. A man stopped by our cabin one afternoon to introduce himself as our neighbor. We knew everyone who had a cabin on the lower creek as they were all friends of Dad's. There was Lloyd up the path on our side of the creek a few hundred yards, after his place was Dan's. Across from Dan's place are Mike and his brother Steve. There had been no one else for all these years, so yes, it was rather strange to us to suddenly have a new neighbor. This was no normal neighbor planning on visiting on the weekends as a getaway from the city. He planned on living there full time on his land.

Hank introduced himself to Dad. He was around Dad's height, had dark hair, and a little aloof from my perspective as a young man. Maybe someone you didn't feel an immediate sense of trust with. Dad was always very cordial to strangers. He always gave them time and the opportunity to talk. He was simply put, always a gentleman. Dad always gave everyone the benefit of doubt and never assumed the worst of anyone unless he had good reason. But, we all remained suspicious and unsure of our new neighbor's intentions.

Hank owned the land directly to the north and up-stream side of us. We had never known who actually owned that land. I had always wondered why no one ever used it. Well now we knew but somehow it didn't really make me, or Dad for that matter, feel any better. The fact is that since he planned on spending a lot more time up there than we were ever going to be able to do, we should make sure that the relationship was good from the start. Dad clearly understood this and was able to secure Hank's cooperation in looking after our place once in a while when he was able.

Mom always thought him to be a "strange recluse" and referred to him as "Hilltop Hank."

Hank had made plans to build a cabin of his own up on the hill back off of the creek about two hundred yards. This was an interesting decision, having put our cabin down near the creek to not only have a great view but also reduce the need to have to carry our gear and supplies a long distance. The other obvious reason was water. We did not want to worry about having to tote our water all the way up the steep hill from the creek. Remember, the only running water in this place is the creek.

Hank's property was actually quite different from ours. Our cabin was built on the northeast edge of our property, about 50 feet from our common property line. There was a very small seasonal stream that joined the creek and formed a natural divider between our property and his. As you followed the small stream back away from the creek towards the hill, the stream would then curve north away from our land and back up into Hank's property. The stream eventually led to a small swamp that lay along the base of the hill. From our cabin towards the streambed, there were no cottonwood trees. Once on Hank's side, there were huge cottonwood trees that seemed at least a hundred feet tall. Some of these trees were no less than 4 feet in diameter, truly giants amongst the small black spruce and alders. One of the interesting elements of foliage was the large ferns. These were huge ferns that covered the landscape between these huge trees. My brother and I used to love to play amongst the ferns when we were younger. They were only a stone's throw from the cabin but gave us the feeling of being in some dense jungle, hunting tigers or looking for the enemy as we played war. These ferns were 6 feet tall and would tower over us. We would find a long strong stick to use as a sword to cut our way through to create a path. Dad made sure he could always see us or at least hear us. I was always very aware of the fact that there were bears around and we could never see one unless we were in its face.

Over the course of the next year, Hank began erecting a fairly rough cabin. He was however a very resourceful man. His cabin was built from logs off of his property like ours but with smaller sized logs, about 5 to 6 inches in diameter. I am assuming this made it easier for him while constructing it himself. This meant many more logs were required to get to the height he desired. The walls were not made of one complete log. They were divided in the middle and anchored to live trees. This is not a wise decision from a construction point of view because if these trees die or continue to grow the structural integrity of the cabin would be damaged. This also created a problem for the cabin to bear the weight of the heavy snow. There was an area towards the front of the cabin that was used as living space and housed a very large cast-iron barrel stove. Towards the rear of the cabin was a small loft for sleeping. The back loft area had a higher roof line that allowed the heat from the stove to be trapped at the area during the cold winter nights. This to me seemed like the one sensible design to the cabin.

Below the loft there was a rather crude kitchen area. What was intriguing to me was the fact that there were no glass windows. Hank had cut out small holes about twelve inches long, one log thick to serve as his windows. There were only two of these in the kitchen area and the rest of the cabin was tightly sealed with solid logs. Hank had also not constructed a set of stairs or porch of any kind to get up to his cabin door, which was up off the ground about 3 feet. I think he must have thought that it would be more difficult for someone or something to get inside his cabin. It was odd because of the length of time he lived there.

Hank took a job during the summer with Mahay's Riverboat Service as a mechanic to help earn enough to live on during the long winter months. Like most of the people who lived in the bush, he was able to get into town with an all terrain vehicle which back then consisted of a 3-wheeler in the summer and with a snowmobile in the winter. Hank must have had the personality type to withstand the quietness and loneliness that living in the wilderness offers. I gave him credit for doing what I knew would be very difficult and probably never try on my own. But then Hank was not your normal guy. He obviously had no family that was dependent on him or other obligations as most people do.

We would see Hank from time to time on our visits to the cabin. It was the end of May in 1987 when I received a phone call from my dad while away at college. Dad said, "You are not going to believe what happened up at the cabin this week," and began recounting the story of how a man (Hank) living in the woods north of Talkeetna was involved in an old fashion gun-fight, supposedly over firewood. As the story goes, according to the *Anchorage Daily News*:

39 year old Henry Clayton and William McCreary, 45, lived about six miles apart, near neighbors in the sparsely settled area of northeast Talkeetna. But in November 1986 McCreary and his wife had fallen out with Clayton over some remarks Clayton made that offended the McCrearys. On May 13, about a quarter after noon the McCrearys reportedly heard a chainsaw at the end of their driveway. They went to investigate, William in the lead and Michelle trailing behind. There they found Clayton cutting wood.

Now you may be thinking this is no big deal. When you live in the woods, trees represent a part of your livelihood, your property, a resource you depend on for many various reasons not to mention the fact that they are a limited resource.

McCreary asked him what he thought he was doing. Clayton answered that he was making a peace offering of firewood.

McCreary told Clayton that he could cut his own firewood and that he didn't need any firewood. He told Clayton to leave them alone.

Clayton reportedly became enraged and said, "You hate people and won't let them do anything for you. I'll give you some violence."

He drew a .44 and shot McCreary in the stomach. McCreary went down, drew his .45, and shot Clayton 6 times – twice in the thigh and 4 times in the abdomen and chest. When the shooting had stopped, McCreary and Clayton lay within 10 feet of each other.

Steve Mahay, of Mahay's Riverboat Service, a widely known local area business, was the medic who got the call from the State Troopers.

"All I was told is that there was a shooting. I didn't know who was shot. This was shortly after another local area shooting where a man had killed several people and took shots at the helicopters that responded. All I could think of was, is this the same type of situation?"

Steve and the State Troopers were dispatched via helicopter to the shooting site where they hovered looking for a landing spot. They were able to land on a small swampy area at the end of the lake near the McCrearys home. They were greeted by a couple of ATVs waiting to take them to the house.

Steve knew Bill McCreary and Hank and was surprised to see them both shot when he arrived.

"While I was attending to Hank's wounds he told me that he had drawn first blood. There was a State Trooper right next to me when he told me."

Steve said they were both pretty bad off and had lost a lot of blood. He was able to get a full account of what happened first hand from Bill's wife and daughter.

They were both evacuated by helicopter. Clayton died in route due to his injuries and McCreary was expected to live after recovering from surgery.

Steve later told me, "I think Hank was surprised to see that Bill had a gun on him. He had reached into his inside coat pocket to pull out his .45 and shoot back at Hank when his gun jammed. This enraged Hank more and he shot at Bill several more times hitting the ground in front of him and hitting Bill a second time in the hip. Bill finally was able to return fire and shot Hank directly in the chest near the heart several times."

"I never knew Hank was capable of something like this" Steve said. "He was always a little quiet and reserved but a good mechanic." Steve had said that he had always liked Hank.

You might think the story would end here. There is some good, though, in all bad things that happen. We went to the cabin shortly after Hank was killed. It was strange to know someone who had actually been shot in a shootout. I asked my dad to take us up to Hank's cabin so we could look around. It had been a long time since I had seen it. Dad agreed and we began the climb up the short hill behind our place. At the top of the hill was a trail that led to Hank's. We looked around and noticed what type of belongings he had there. I wondered who would come to take care of all his things. I asked my dad and he said, "No one, they will probably all be gone in a week or two once the word makes it around that he is gone." "Do you mean that people will steal all his things?" I asked my dad. "Yes, unfortunately out here there is little you can do to keep that from happening," said Dad.

Over that summer we made many trips to our cabin. Each time I would take the short hike up to Hank's place to check on things. Every time there would be more things missing. The snow mobile and 3-wheeler were the first things to go. He had many things stored around the cabin and under it. Hank had also built a crude form of what you would call a cache. This was to store things at an elevated level to keep the bears and other critters out of your supplies. Most of these things were now gone.

The cabin had been broken into and many things missing. This did however allow an investigative young man like myself to have a glimpse into Hank's world. There were magazines everywhere. Large containers of various types of cooking essentials had been opened and their contents spilled across the cabin floor. The place was a mess to put it lightly. I spent a few minutes looking around and taking notice of how he must have lived in this solitude.

Several years had passed and my sister Carrie had taken the time to look into who owned the land that Hank's cabin was on. She was able to determine his dad; living in the lower 48 was the owner. Carrie made contact with him, explained that she was the daughter of the man who owned the property next to his and our story. She made the man an offer for the land and he accepted. As it turned out, he owned the five acres next to Dad and the five acres directly behind it. My sister is not your average woman. She had plans for this old run-down poor excuse for a cabin. Together with her friend, they bought 4-wheelers and cut a trail to her new property. Over the next few summers the rundown cabin turned into a new-looking structure and a perfect little getaway in the woods for her and her two children Anthony and Alexia.

The cabin was made out of logs but over the years the front half of the cabin had collapsed under the pressure of the snow. The logs had to be cut out and moved to the side. Carrie then built a new wall and put in windows. This made the cabin significantly smaller than the original but sufficient for her needs. Last summer she added a nice wood wrap-around deck to the front of the cabin.

Carrie's Cabin after much work and renovation

There are a few leftover souvenirs of Hank's past life. The remains of his old huge solid steel barrel stove still sit out front. I don't know that it will ever be moved as heavy as it is. It lies amongst the weeds and grass as a steadfast reminder of what was once there. Like a monument, of sorts, to the old dwelling that once housed Hank.

Chapter 11
Extreme Winter

"A snowflake is one of God's most fragile creations, but look what
they can do when they stick together!"
-Author Unknown

Winter in Alaska can be extreme. The elements can wreak
havoc on anything. The cold and snow with constant thawing
and freezing cause many different challenges when building.
Our cabin is no exception. It was the winter of 1990 when one
of the largest snow falls on record hit the area of Talkeetna.

According to the Old Farmers Almanac, on February 12,
1990, it was -41.3°F, clear with over 30 miles visibility for the day.
The snow depth measurement for the day was 39.80 inches or 3
feet deep. This was one of the coldest days recorded for the
winter. Snowfall had been above average so far for the year.

Cold weather and Alaska are somewhat synonymous. There are however not many places people live where the temperature drops to -50°F and with the wind chill even colder. You have to be very well equipped and prepared for the extreme of what nature has to offer. Those who choose to live in a beautiful area like Talkeetna know and understand this.

The weather becomes the main factor you have to contend with. The river slowly drops in depth and in volume as fall fades into the winter months. The water tends to become quite clear, not showing the same level of silt that you see in the warmer summer months. The cold slowly starts to creep its way across the water as if it were some unseen mystical force, slowly devouring everything in its path. Time seems to start to slow. Ice soon encapsulates the entire surface of what was once a raging river. Snow provides the necessary insulating blanket to enable the ice to continue to form and thicken its hold on the river.

Ice is fully capable, as we all know, of forming on moving water like a river with the right conditions. Even during the depth of the winter, one is still able to find small open pockets of water, never grasped by the cold enough to form an ice covering. The process that each water molecule goes through to form ice crystals that ultimately make solid ice masses is truly a mystery. Many a scientist and mathematician have spent countless hours and have built beautiful algorithms to help us gain insight into this. If you stare at these long enough they actually begin to look like ice crystals themselves. I like to believe that nature and the laws that govern her, have an ultimate creator that fully understands every atomic aspect to this and is fully in control of it. As a result, I tend to not loose too much sleep over this issue. I do enjoy looking at the beautiful formations that appear in a land ruled by the river.

Towards the end of February of 1990, the snow began to fall and not let up for several days. By March 6, 1990, according to the Old Farmers Almanac, there was 80 inches of snow recorded on the ground. To put this into perspective for those of us who are somewhat mathematically challenged, this is 6 feet 6 inches in total depth.

Winter was always a beautiful time to go to the cabin. First was the adventure of having to get to the cabin on snowmobiles instead of by boat. This always proved to be interesting and challenging, not unlike many of the boat trips.

The trek was one of two ways; we were either able to go up the river or we had to go cross country via the railroad tracks and backcountry trail.

The river route was always quite unsettling to me as a young man. I had read so many stories of people falling through the ice on snowmobiles, whether on a lake or river, and drowning, that it was always hard for me to enjoy unless we were on the river bank. There was never a trail this way. One would have to basically make his own.

This required a lead snowmobile that was light and good at breaking trail. The heavier machines would then follow on the established track. Trail riding can be very difficult on snow. The trail is usually winding and through trees. As a result you are not able to go very fast. If you happen to fall off the trail, it is very easy to then get stuck.

When I was younger, I was very capable at driving a snowmobile but lacked the strength to lift one. When I would get stuck, it always meant that I needed my dad's help. This meant lifting the skis up and then lifting the back end up while trying to power out of the hole and back onto the trail. It was difficult and strenuous work in deep snow. Dad was usually exhausted by the time we would reach the cabin.

First order of business was usually digging an entrance to the door of the cabin. The front of the cabin was usually much lower than where the snowmobiles would be. We would have to

use a shovel kept at the back of the cabin to dig steps down and dig the entry to the door. Once opened, we would then start a fire in the stove to get things warmed up. The cabin is pretty well insulated and would be colder than an icebox inside. The windows would then need to be cleared of snow and the boards taken off so that some natural light would be able to penetrate into the interior.

The front of the cabin with Chris and his friend after digging an entrance down through the snow.

The days are short during the winter in Alaska. The sun is usually not up till around mid morning and would then go back down in the early afternoon. We spent a lot of time in the cabin just relaxing and playing games. There were some chores to be done but not nearly as many as in the summer. The main thing to do was keep the fire going in the cabin. Firewood is very hard to come by in the middle of winter. With some forethought this can be made much easier. The trick is to make sure that plenty has been cut the summer before and stacked and covered to allow easy access.

As a kid, the only thing I wanted to do was drive the snowmobiles around. My dad and I would make trails around the cabin like a race track and once they had been driven on a few times and packed down it was much easier for my brother and me to navigate. The favorite ride was a short trail back up to a lake that allowed the real need for speed every young boy has to be unleashed. Once on the open snow, you were free to run the machine at full throttle and literally sail across the top of the snow. The cold air mixed with the flying snow would bite into your face unlike anything you had ever felt. Even with goggles my eyes would tear up so bad I couldn't see a thing. This also helped me conquer my fear of falling through the ice, never to be found again. There were times when the lake would have overflow and you could find yourself riding through water that was trapped on top of the ice. I would have to say that is about the scariest feeling next to actually falling through the ice that I experienced. Occasionally you could hear the ice pop and crack as you sped across the top of it. I always thought if I just kept going fast enough I could outrun it and be out of danger.

The nights were cold and illuminated by the beautiful starlit skies. The northern lights would dance across horizon as if performing just for you. It was quiet, oh so quiet, with the blanket of snow somehow muffling every noise. The snow was crisp and crunched under your feet when you walked. The sound of water could still be heard flowing under the ice blanket on top. Winter was a time of solitude and everything seemed to move in slow motion.

One memorable year the snowfall had been particularly deep.

My dad had to spend much more time shoveling than normal. Snow was so deep that the stove pipe had to be dug out on top of the cabin. The snow was as high as the eves on the roof of the cabin.

View of the snow amassed on the cabin roof

With that much weight on top it was necessary to shovel as much off as possible. So Dad began to shovel away and when he finished, he was able to ride his snowmobile right over the cabin as if it were merely a small hill in the way.

The backside of the cabin

I was always amazed at the structural integrity the old log cabin had. I am not mathematician but the weight of the mass of that snow had to be enormous. How it hasn't collapsed after all these years is only a testament to my dad's ingenuity and engineering.

Dad driving his snowmobile over the top of the cabin

The type of wildlife seen in the wintertime varies quite a bit from what is normally seen during the summer months. Small furry creatures are more prevalent, like mink, marten, otter, beaver, and fox. Bears are not a threat this time of year as they are fast asleep in their warm den, waiting and dreaming of warmer months and slaying salmon. Moose can still be seen, nibbling on the tree branches and digging for vegetation beneath the snow. Wolves would have to be the main predator of the winter months as they travel through the area seeking an easy meal from some calf or sick cow moose.

*View of the creek downstream with the snowmobiles parked
at the edge of the creek bank*

The river remains that sleeping giant as it flows endlessly under the snow and ice, working its way to its final destination, the ocean. The level of water is much lower during the winter months than it is in the summer time.

When the weather starts to warm and the snow and ice begins to melt, water once again becomes the never-ending dominant force. It carves and scrapes and devours anything in

its path. The ice breaks with a deafening roar and carries with it anything left in its path. Once again the waters are clear and the salmon begin their journey upstream to their ancient spawning grounds to recreate the cycle of life they started many years ago.

The outhouse

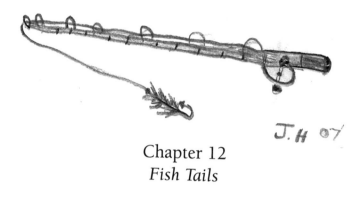

J. H 07

Chapter 12
Fish Tails

"A man's fish tale is like a weed in your grass,
both never stop growing."
-BPH

No book about Alaska would be complete without some great stories about fishing. After all, fishing is as much a part of life in Alaska as snow or ice. When you talk with someone about Alaska from the lower 48, one of the first things they ask is about the fishing. I was blessed with the opportunity to go fishing on a regular basis with my dad. We were fortunate enough to live in a place that had great fishing. Over the years there are a few stories that stand out more than the rest. Some include fish; some are simply stories that include fishing but no fish. Either way they were all somehow intertwined around the same main character, the river.

In the early days of trips up the river, it was still a remote destination and only a handful of people would be seen either daring to navigate the river or fishing along its path. There was and still is a very good fishing spot at the mouth of Clear Creek where it joins the mighty Talkeetna River. In the old days this was considered the old mouth of the creek as only a small amount of water entered the river. The real mouth of the creek was a quarter of a mile upstream. The irony of that is that it has now changed back due to the flood. Here there is a large bend in the river and a large sand bar to stand on while fishing.

When I was a kid, we would stop here and fish for kings in the hole where they lay before they made their journey upstream.

On one occasion I caught over 50 salmon. They were mostly pinks and were easy to catch. I would have fun reeling them in then remove the hook and set them free. Dad enjoyed watching us kids catch fish and ended up spending more time helping us than fishing himself. A fate that I too have found while trying to fish with my 10-year-old son. After landing one of the many large male "humpies" that day, I remember putting him back in the water. I held him upright the way Dad taught me until he swam off under his own strength. The only problem was he didn't just swim off like every other salmon I had caught that day. I happened to be standing in about 12 inches of water and noticed that this salmon began to circle my legs as if telling me that he was somehow thankful for what I had just done. After a few circles he disappeared back into the deep water and I stood there as an amazed 8 year old would. I wondered why that fish had just done that. I told my dad but noticed he too had been watching and seen what the fish had done. I felt a certain connection and respect for the fish. I thought to myself that I must somehow be special. For some reason that fish chose me.

It was memory that stayed with me and that I thought about sharing someday when I would write a book.

When I was a kid, my dad would often allow me to bring a friend up to the cabin for the weekend. He felt very strongly about sharing what we had with others might not have a dad that shared the same passion for the outdoors or that chose to not take the time to spend engaging in those types of activities. On one occasion I remember bringing a friend from school who didn't get a chance to go out fishing much and was very excited at the idea of going to this cabin he had been hearing about.

Nick was a great baseball player but not a very good fisherman. We had fun around the cabin but were really excited to catch some good fish. We were in the sixth grade and for kids our age we might as well been in heaven. One afternoon while fishing, Nick managed to get a large hook jammed into his finger. Now I don't really recall how he did this and I am sure he is probably happy that I don't but I don't really think it matters how he did it, only that he did. As you can imagine, he was in a tremendous amount of pain.

This unfortunate experience put a damper on our fishing. The problem is that the only way to get a barbed hook out of the flesh of your finger is to push it the rest of the way through and cut off the barb. Then, as if that is not enough pain, the hook can then be pulled back through the original hole. Ouch! It makes me sick just thinking about it. Dad was troubled by this and wasn't sure if we should make the trip out to get Nick to a doctor or what we should do. In fact I think he left it up to Nick to decide. Being a little out of his comfort zone with someone else's child, Dad decided to go across the creek to Steve's cabin for some counsel.

The prognosis wasn't good and basically consisted of having to push the hook through to cut the barb. To his credit, Nick was extremely brave and tough for a boy his age. He managed to survive the procedure and spent the rest of the weekend taking it easy. I am sure that this was one accident that he did not want to remember but yet will have been emblazed on his mind forever.

Below the cabin, downstream a few hundred yards, was a large log jam. At this point there is a small amount of water that flows down what once was a channel for the creek. Under the log jam was a large beaver hut. The water was deep and created a nice hole for the fish. The logs were huge and provided a way to maneuver out over the hole to fish directly above it while missing most of the potential snags. The walk from the cabin is about 10 minutes and just in view from the creek bank in front. Dad would allow us kids to occasionally walk down there without him. It was a long walk through the brush along the creek. As a kid it was a very scary walk. At that distance there was nothing Dad could do if a bear threatened us. We were on our own. That did not stop me from making the trek hundreds of times in the hope of catching a nice fish.

On one sunny Saturday I made the walk down to the beaver dam to fish. I was still young, maybe around 12. I knew how to fish this spot and enjoyed sitting out over the water on a log while trying to hook a fish. I would glance upstream every so often, just checking to see if Dad was looking or not. It always somehow made me feel a little safer if he was out there. The kings were running and I could see them schooled up under the logs in the hole. I marveled at their size. They seemed as large as me. This day I was not equipped to catch one of those monsters, I was after the large trout that enjoy following the salmon and eat their eggs.

Dad enjoying a sunny day at the beaver dam hole

I could peer down into the crystal clear water and see every fish. I knew where the kings were and where the darker smaller bodies that followed them were. Flashes of red would dart under me as the salmon would chase away the trout or a rival. I had my favorite spinning lure fastened to my line and planned on catching the biggest one I could find. While I sat on the log with line in hand watching the salmon, something jumped out of the water at my pole. This just about sent me tumbling over the log and into the water. As I sat there to regain my composure it happened again. I soon realized that my lure had been dangling just above the water's surface and that the bright reflection of the sun made it appear as an appetizing meal to the large rainbow trout that had just lunged at it. This time I was ready and held my rod tightly. I made sure to dangle the lure just at the surface enabling the fish to have a slightly easier time catching its prey. Much to my surprise it worked. With a sudden pounce, that fish surfaced and hit my lure with a mighty "thwack." My rod tip bent like a noodle and the fight was on. I was amazed at the strength this fish had and wondered could it really be a trout. I had to maneuver myself back down the log while fighting this fish, across several other logs and over to a small sand bar where I planned to land it. I didn't have a net so hoped my strategy worked. A few short minutes later I had a 20-inch rainbow trout flopping on shore. Boy was I proud. Dad would never believe me when I told him how I had caught this hog. I practically ran all the way back carrying my prize and beaming with excitement. Dad smiled and listened as I told my tale. He was skeptical I'm sure, but nonetheless was happy for me. I didn't care if he believed me or not as I knew what had happened. I hadn't been seeing things. That trout jumped out of the creek on that beautiful sunny day and right onto my hook before I had even lowered it into the water. I just figured that was one hungry fish.

One time fishing for salmon, again at the old mouth on the sand bar, one of the funniest things I have yet seen fishing happened. When the salmon are running in the river you can tell. The air smells different. It reeks of fish. There are dead salmon everywhere. They are in the water, on the beach, stuck on limbs and branches. As a result, it also tends to bring out the scavengers that inhabit the area. Despite being inland over a hundred miles, there are sea gulls everywhere. The gulls know where to find food and don't seem to mind being that far away from the ocean.

There were several of us fishing that day and we were spread out across the edge of the sand bar. The salmon were in just thick, so we were just slaying fish that day.

If I remember things accurately it was my brother Scott who

somehow, while casting his line, happened to hook a sea gull in mid air! This made for quite an interesting sight as he did not know what to do but start reeling it in. Dad was quite alarmed and worried about someone from fish and game being there and getting in trouble. I remember laughing my head off watching my brother reel in a bird. The gull did not come willingly. It took some time to coax it close enough to shore to figure out what had happened. Luckily the line had looped around the bird and the hook had actually hooked on the line and made a lasso of sorts around the bird. This was good news as it wasn't hooked or injured from the hook itself. Dad grabbed the bird and held it down enough to get the line untangled and free the bird. Everyone watching cheered as the bird took flight and I am assuming decided he had enough river fishing and headed back home to the sea.

Dad was a good fisherman. He was the kind of person who just seemed to have the knack to catch fish. He would always catch fish even on days when no one else would. He really enjoyed himself and spent much time fishing. He was however not a purist. He was a sport meat fisher.

He believed in catching fish to eat them. It didn't matter to him what kind of pole, reel, or hook he had on at the time. As long as it was legal he would use

Dad with a nice silver salmon

it. This included some unorthodox methods over the years that seem to come and then go as fast as they came.

One practical application that we used for many years was to help keep the salmon eggs on the hook. Fishing for kings could be done many ways but what Dad liked best was using salmon egg clusters. Every year we would make sure to keep enough salmon eggs from that year from our catch to ensure we had enough for the following year. Much time and preparation went into ensuring their future. They were cleaned and cured on newspaper with good old-fashioned Borax powder soap. This helped the egg sacks dry and seal together well for attaching to the hook. The eggs were then placed in zip lock bags and frozen for next year.

In the early years we would use large treble hooks with a weight and nothing more to catch kings. The method consisted of cutting a small chunk of cured salmon eggs and hooking it over the hooks in one nice big juicy clump. This was the best recipe for catching fish. But one flaw existed and that was the ability to keep the eggs on the hook for more than a few minutes. Yes, there was a commercial solution designed for this but that cost money.

Dad was too thrifty for that and decided that old panty hose would do the trick. So, he would cut small sections of Mom's old hose into squares and use it to drape over the eggs and onto the hooks. This acted as a bag around the eggs but yet still allowed the smell of the eggs to penetrate into the water to attract the fish. I was always embarrassed at the idea of using Mom's old hose to fish but Dad didn't seem to let it bother him a bit.

Dad with a nice king salmon in 1972

Chapter 13
Bear Tales I

"A strong body makes the mind strong. As to the species of exercises, I advise the gun. While this gives moderate exercise to the body, it gives boldness, enterprise, and independence to the mind...

"Let your gun therefore be the constant companion of your walks."
-Thomas Jefferson

Alaska is home to the world's largest carnivores, the Alaskan grizzly bear. The close cousin to the grizzly is the brown bear. These tend to be mostly coastal area bears and grow larger than inland grizzlies. Their habitat ranges from the Brooks Range in northern Alaska down through Canada and into the northern states in the lower 48.

Grizzlies can range in size from 500 lbs. to 1,500 lbs. The largest of the grizzlies in North America tend to be in Alaska due to the abundant supply of food. These carnivores are also avid vegetarians in that they love to eat berries. Wherever you have lots of fresh fish and berries, there you will find grizzlies.

There is also another close relative of the grizzly, the Alaskan black bear. The black bears cohabitate with the grizzly in the area where our cabin is. Smaller in size, the black bear can also be just as dangerous and is often underestimated in a close encounter.

Bears tend to be mainly nocturnal creatures and usually do not pose too large of a problem during the daytime. They do not like the heat and prefer a lot of cover to the wide open. During the daytime they would just as soon be in their bed and do their fishing in the evening.

There have been many times over the years when we have seen bears up at the cabin. It tends to be a fairly regular occurrence. Most of our bear sightings are at a fairly comfortable distance. They tend to be sighted in the early evening when we are all gathered around the campfire in front of the cabin. Most times they are black bears on the far side of the creek walking the creek bank. As soon as they see or hear us they usually disappear into the brush and are never seen again.

There are however times when they get too close for our comfort and we are on as I like to say "high alert." It is a little strange that over the years we tend to see more bears than we ever used to when I was younger. For this reason we go nowhere without a gun. Usually a 12-guage shotgun loaded with bear slug. My dad also has a .454 Casual, one of the most powerful handguns available today. One never knows when it will be necessary to protect oneself. Like the quote at the beginning of the chapter, there is a sense of companionship with a gun. Out in the wilderness is the only time you can walk around with a gun on your hip without worrying about what someone else may think or say. There is a liberating feeling of self security and a romantic tie to past when the early pioneers actually did carry their guns on their person everywhere they went. Thomas Jefferson obviously related to this concept and so do I. Without it you sooner or later end up like the Grizzly Man, bear food.

Because of the many stories we have I have decided to pick a few that stick out in my mind and experience more than others. If I included them all, I would have to write a separate book about this one subject.

One of Dad's

One story I recall from Dad was an encounter he had with Lloyd during one of his early adventures at Clear Creek. They were going down the creek at a slow idle. It was a calmer part of the creek, down an old slough which is no longer passable. This part of the creek was extremely narrow and only 15-feet wide. Rounding a corner they ran right into a large grizzly sow with a set of cubs in the middle of the stream. There was no way to stop. As the boat approached the men were ready for a certain encounter. The bears moved quickly to the side of the stream. As they went by there was no more than 10 feet separating them. Suddenly the sow charged, lunging toward the boat and men. As fast as it charged it stopped, just only a few feet away, scaring them out of their shorts. Bears often do this to test their ground and establish dominance. Luckily they passed unscathed and lived to tell the story to all.

Steve Kurth's Tales

Our neighbor and good friend Steve Kurth has a cabin on the other side of the creek from ours and upstream about a quarter

of a mile. Steve is an avid hunter and someone that my dad and I have hunted with many times over the years. Unlike Steve, my dad did not like to hunt for moose around the cabin due to the many grizzly bears. He was not inclined to put his kids in harm's way even when they were armed. Now I have to admit that there were times when I talked my dad into taking me hunting around the cabin for moose. We were never successful but also never hunted the area hard.

Steve was more daring and determined to get a moose. I specifically remember one encounter that he had with grizzly bears that stuck in my mind.

Steve was hunting with his brother-in-law and they were fortunate to get a bull moose. Steve recalled, "That was my biggest bull moose at 62 inches." He told me how they were able to get the meat packed out. But when his brother learned about his success, he wanted the hide.

So Steve said that regretfully, they went back to the kill site to retrieve the hide.

Early the next morning they went back for the hide. The kill was in very heavy grass and brush. The ground has many soft spots between large clumps of grass and moss. These are known as hummocks and are most commonly seen on the open tundra or near swamps and lakes. There is always a lot of swampy, boggy, wet low-lying area to contend with. This makes it extremely difficult to walk quietly and makes it very slow walking.

Upon arriving near the kill zone, the men were confronted with a large grizzly that heard them approaching and had stood on his hind quarters to take a look. When you see a grizzly standing up, you know instantly you are in for trouble. The reason they stand is to get a better scent on their prey. Grizzlies have extremely poor eyesight. Many people do not know this. They rely very heavily on their smelling senses for danger and prey and do not have very good eye-sight. This grizzly had obviously found the gut pile from the moose and it meant an easy morning meal. Steve told me that they both turned to run but fell down on their backs. Now Steve is an experienced hunter and knows that he cannot outrun a grizzly. Grizzlies have incredible speed and can outrun a quarter horse in the first quarter of a mile. I, too, know this from experience. I have seen a grizzly run when it was in the open area off the end of a lake that was so difficult for us to cover that it took over 30 minutes in an ATV. This bear I saw on a hunting trip with my dad and brother ran like it was being chased and covered this same distance in less than a minute.

They are so massively fast they trample anything in their path and let nothing slow them down.

Steve said that the grizzly charged them and stopped only five feet away. He remembered seeing the grass move at his feet from the bear's charge. He lay there quietly while the bear retreated, gun in hand waiting to shoot if need be.

After he was sure it left, they found the first tree they could climb to wait for another hour or two until they were sure they were safe. Steve chuckled to himself while recounting his story.

He said, "I sure regret going back there for that hide; that sure was stupid of us."

He told me one other story he remembered well about running into a grizzly. He was moose hunting back behind Strid's cabin with a friend from Iowa. They were near the base of a small hill and in a clearing with nothing higher than their knees. He said it was mostly blueberries.

Steve turned and thought he saw a moose when he realized that it had much too short of legs to be a moose. He quickly realized it was a grizzly and before he knew it, the griz charged from 20 yards away. It came crashing through the brush down the small hill and suddenly stopped only 5 yards away! I asked him why he didn't shoot it and he said he would have had it got a little closer. Steve said, "That grizzly wasn't real happy with us being there." He turned back up the hill a few yards, ripping up brush with his paws and then turned and charged a second time! Luckily he did the same thing, he stopped, turned and disappeared into the brush. Steve said he had a total of four close encounters with grizzlies while hunting around the area. That is four more than I want.

Another Steve Tale

This story is about a friend of my sister's also named Steve. He had been helping my sister Carrie with work on her cabin which is located just above ours on the small hill behind us. Steve was up during the week bringing some supplies and doing some work. They use four-wheelers to access her property. This is a fun trip that begins in the town of Talkeetna. From Talkeetna they follow the railroad tracks north for a few miles before heading east through the woods on a system of trails. Many people live back in the woods with no road access. They access their property with four-wheelers in the summer and snowmobiles in the winter. Carrie and Steve had built a trail to get to their property from Talkeetna in about two and a half hour's ride. My sister's cabin seems to be right on a bear trail. There are many times a black bear will walk right in front of her cabin while we are inside. Most of these sightings are at night. The loft is where the sleeping quarters are and sits above the living area. There is a window overlooking the front area of her cabin and it is here that the bears seem to happen by.

Steve was on his way down the trail that runs across the top of the hill before dropping a steep 50 feet towards our cabin. From the top of this hill you can see the sauna and cabin quite well. As he approached the beginning of the downward trail, he noticed something near the sauna.

My dad has always been very aware of the bears in the area. He knows the power and strength of these animals. I learned from a very early age to have the highest level of respect for bears. I have never hunted them despite having ample opportunity to do so. I was never excited by the chance of walking up on a grizzly 20 feet away with nothing but one shot and luck on my side. That is what you would need to hunt in this part of Alaska. There is just far too much cover to overcome and they are the masters of this domain. As a result, Dad would always cut the grass around the cabin back for at least 50 to 75 yards so that we could at least see anything that might approach. Brush and small trees were also cleared so that it was fairly open behind and to the sides of the cabin. Once past the sauna area which was back behind about 50 yards it was natural growth. This included much of the hillside area behind the cabin.

What Steve saw is a sight that one would normally not see in a lifetime. Next to the sauna in the grass were five grizzlies all bedded down. Steve was armed with a .44 caliber handgun. This gun probably has enough shells to stop a grizzly if you were lucky. It certainly was not enough to stop five if need be. Steve was not about to come down the hill to my dad's cabin with these bears there. He removed his pistol and fired a shot in the air hoping to scare them away. Much to his dismay they did not move. He fired another shot. Other than a few of them looking around it did not garner any of the desired results After a third shot two of them got up, noticeably disturbed. Steve then realized that left him with only a few more rounds and that the odds were definitely not in his favor. He slowly retreated, and went back the direction he came from, yielding to the very precarious situation he found himself in. We have never seen more than one grizzly at any time at the cabin. One can only imagine why there were five all in the same location and why they had chosen the inconspicuous location for their nap that day.

Chapter 14:
Bear Tales II

"A close encounter with a bear in the wild will be an image burned
into your memory like no other; always to be remembered."
-BPH

Moms Tale

In the summer of 1994, Mom and Dad had invited some
guests, to come up to Alaska, not unlike every other summer, to
enjoy a memorable experience at the Horacek cabin. In
preparation for so many people staying in our small cabin they
planned how they could make it work and be comfortable for all,
what foods were needed, and the gear and equipment they would
need to take. Several trips up the river would be necessary to get
everyone and everything up there for the few days' stay. Their
plan was simple: Take the gear up to the cabin, off load it, Dad
leaves Mom at the cabin to get things in order and he heads back
downstream to town to pick up the guests.

Over all the years of venturing beyond the normal bounds of civilization, going into what I call the wilderness, Mom's fear had not been so much encountering bears up close and personal, nor was it getting stranded on the riverside. My mom had made it through going up to our property and cabin on the river for over 30 years, and usually with five children. She had learned to trade most of her little fears for caution. In spite of having years of exposure, she had to own the long-suppressed fear of finding herself alone in the wilderness. This trip however, would be her first real planned challenge to this anxiety. Mom was always comforted by the reality that it was only going to be an hour or two. She knew Dad would always return for her. Besides, she actually liked the challenge it presented.

Her second biggest fear though had always been encountering a bear while alone in the wilderness. Armed with all the knowledge shared by the most experienced of wilderness travelers on what to do if one encounters bears and armed with a weapon that has a shell for any occasion, she seldom visited this potential opportunity or fear. No one particularly wants to cross paths with a bear, black or grizzly, be it only paces away or a hundred yards away.

Mom and Dad made it up to the cabin, not without their own usual outboard motor challenges. With gear scattered on the upper banks, Mom had Dad show her again how to fire up the gas-powered trimmer to cut the grass in front of the cabin. This helps alleviate some fear as it makes a lot of noise. Critters don't like it and are more inclined to give us space and a wide berth when passing by. It was the weed whacker or the chain-saw; either was equally loud and effective.

Why was my mom so preoccupied with bears? I think in part because they are quite plentiful and she is no one's fool. She understands the potential risks they represent. Regardless, having thought it all through, she was nonetheless prepared to stay that short while by herself. Mom commented on how that reality was somehow empowering. She knew where this sense of confidence came from and embraced those feelings as she waved goodbye to Dad at around 4 p.m. After all, he would be back soon with their company and it stays light until midnight.

The first order of business was to open up the cabin, take all the window covers off, and stow the food and gear. Next was to build a fire, as it keeps mosquitoes and critters at a distance; then cut the grass. The tall grass always bugged her and cutting it makes walking about easier, and it cuts down on the insects. After countless pulls, sputters, and false starts, she finally got the trimmer started and was able to cut the 10-inch-tall grass in the front of the cabin, until the fuel finally ran out. After finishing, she began to wonder where Dad and the guests were. They should have been back by this time as it was approaching 8 p.m.

By then she figured Dad must have had major motor problems and she was worried about him being alone on the river with a bad motor. If they didn't get back by 10 p.m. or so, he'd likely hold off navigating the river until the morning when the light is better. That is when it struck her, "I AM HERE ALONE" and "I will be spending all night ALONE in the wilderness." As she piled a few more large logs on the fire, she decided to not cook the food she had planned for dinner. Internally, she reflected on the fact that she would be spending the night alone, albeit in a stout log cabin with a solid thick plank wood door. Surely she would be fine and there was nothing to really worry about.

Mom rose early that next morning, realizing she was still by herself, stuck at the cabin. No boats had come up the creek as the king salmon were not yet running. It was a quiet morning, the sky was clear, and the birds were chirping in a cheerful song of early morning awakening. She fixed some coffee, her normal morning ritual, and had something to eat.

Later Mom opened the wood door and closed the screen door behind her to let the fresh morning air in the cabin. By 8 a.m. there was still no sign of anyone. She thought "What good is a cell phone if those you need to contact don't have one too." Mom wondered what could be going on downstream. Why wasn't Dad back yet? What were her cousins thinking about as they lay stranded on some lone sandbar on the river.

As she stood by the front window sipping her coffee, mentally communing with nature, she observed the stream flowing gently by, a large bald eagle gliding to a treetop on the far side of the creek, and a merganser duck with several little ones skittering around the rocks. It was much like watching the nature channel on a big screen TV.

In front of the cabin, the creek is about 8 feet below the steep bank's edge. We had constructed some crude earthen steps, or I should say my mom had, to make climbing the incline easier. It was up these steps that a large furry face appeared, then next an upper body, followed by a big grizzly-looking bruin. "How fascinating," she thought, as he stopped at the top of the bank, looked left, right, then sniffed the air. He was broad-cheeked, broad-necked and big shouldered, but very dark in color. This was interesting until she realized that all there was between him and her was 30 feet of grass and a screen door! Still watching for what seemed like several minutes, but was only a matter of seconds, he took a couple of steps to his right towards Dad's favorite seat and it was then she got a good look at his full girth and decided "That is one BIG BEAR, I'd better do something." The gun was hanging by the cabin door, always ready, always handy, so quietly she took two side steps towards it, lifting it off its peg. The shotgun still had a shell in the chamber from the night before so she carefully flipped off the safety, estimating she had enough time to ready the gun by her right hip while grabbing the screen door with her left hand. Just then the bear realized she was there.

This is a much smaller bear than the one Mom saw

Heart racing, adrenalin pumping, she reached for the door and that's when a voice inside her said, "This is when you are suppose to yell." Knowing this was a weapon she could wield quite well, she shouted in her loudest and most intimidating voice, telling that bruin to, "Get out of here." She didn't get the door shut fast enough before she saw that BIG critter literally jump a few feet off the ground, somersaulting backwards over the 8-foot-creek bank and disappeared out of sight.

Mom didn't know if the sweat she wiped on her shirtsleeve was due to hot flashes or anxiety, but just like in the movies, there she stood, back against the door breathing a long sigh of relief. In an emotional release she started laughing at herself. Not wishing to become overconfident, she proceeded to find something to make a lot more noise than her yell. There was nothing better than the old heavy aluminum cabin pots in the kitchen. They became her cymbals and she the first chair in the philharmonic orchestra. She banged them with vigor, declaring that "breakfast was over and she wasn't going to be any critter's brunch." Mom chuckled again to herself, thinking, "No one will ever believe this."

Shortly thereafter, she heard that familiar sound of what she knew was Dad's boat roaring up the creek. Mom figured Dad had to drive back to Anchorage to get his other motor while his cousins and guests waited anxiously for Captain Chuck to return and ferry them up to their adventure on Clear Creek at the Horacek cabin.

My Bear Tale

On my last trip in 2004, it was our ritual sauna night. We had all made our first dip in the creek to cool off from the heat. My nephew, Anthony, was ready for another trip. No one else was taking advantage of this opportunity so I reluctantly agreed. After reheating in the sauna for another 10 minutes, we slipped on our sandals, grabbed a towel and made our mad dash for the creek. I ran for it at full speed. It is a good 75 yards to the creek, straight past the fire pit area with the spectators hooting and a hollering their encouragement. Down the small decline towards the creek and after dropping my towel, in I went. Normally I wouldn't be ahead of my nephew but this time I was. I had done this a hundred times, at least, in my life. Each time is a different rush. The cold water is somewhat shocking at first toe dip. Just wading up to your knee does not qualify for this family ritual. One must fully submerge, swim with the salmon, a self-baptism of sorts, the Clear Creek way.

I had no need to think this was going to be any different than every other time I had done this. As I entered the water, naked as a jay bird before God and his beautiful creation, I soon realized that I was not alone. I ran smack into a huge Alaskan grizzly bear! The bear was directly across the creek from me at a distance of 20 yards.

He belted out an intimidating roar as loud as a furry freight train and bolted back into the dense brush along that side of the

Grizzly directly across the creek from the cabin much like that night, without as much light.

creek. It was then, standing in the water knee deep, naked to the world, facing this huge grizzly, that my heart about jumped out of my body, this time not from the cold creek. Needless to say I did not linger there long. I was back up the bank with my nephew as fast as I could move. I had let out the expected alarm to camp by yelling "Bearrrrrr!" No one needed that help as they heard the bear as loud as I did. Back at the sauna, the guys had also heard the ruckus and came up to investigate. My body, full of pumping adrenalin, told them what happened. I wasn't able to settle down for bed that evening until another drink or two to help settle the nerves. That had been my closest personal experience with a bear at our cabin in the last 30 years. What a tale I had to tell the kids when I returned home.

Bear Break-In

Bears are by nature very curious animals. They are driven by their natural desires, like most animals. The strongest of these is to consume as much as they can before the winter months come.

The closer to winter, the more driven they are. When the salmon run is not as large as they are used to, it drives them to find alternative sources of nourishment.

One of the routines we have devised over the years to help deter any unwanted visitors in our cabin is to make sure it is locked up tight when we leave. This involves not only securing the front door from unwanted guests but also making sure the windows are boarded. Bears have such a sensitive sense of smell they can smell food miles away. This includes food in a cabin. The easiest path of entry is obviously a window. As a result we have to board up the windows to keep them out. This has to be done in a way that will not allow them the ability to grab anything with their claws. We have learned this lesson the hard way. In the early years, we would simply put up a board on the window. That had proved to not be effective. There have been times when a bear has literally ripped the board off and broken out the window to gain access to the inside of the cabin. Once in they make a mess unlike any animal you could imagine. This has happened on several occasions. My dad was not deterred by this in the least. He devised a way to screw boards that would not allow any grip for the animal. We thought that all would surely be safe and secure. Several years passed without an unwanted intruder making a mess and causing the necessary replacement of a window. That is until the bears figured out another way in.

When you have a cabin for as many years as we have you continually find ways to improve and enhance things to make life more comfortable. This may include things like better ways to heat and light the interior. One of these stokes of genius was to add a skylight to allow more natural light in the cabin. We had cut a hole in the roof between two of the rafter logs and installed a skylight about 2 by 3 feet. What a difference it made. Everyone loved the new addition.

One summer upon returning to the cabin we opened the front door only to find monumental mess on the cabin floor. Everything that had any food in it was literally chewed open and spilled on the floor. This mess consisted of pancake mix, flour, coffee, sugar, rice and any other staple you could think of. Not to mention the many chewed open cans of beer and soda pop. Some acrobatic bear had climbed onto the roof, ripped off the skylight and some how lowered itself into the cabin. After

Black bear crossing the creek near the cabin

having its fill it also had figured out how to acrobatically climb its way back out the gapping hole it left in the roof.

This is not the way you want to start a quiet weekend at the family cabin. The remainder of the weekend was spent cleaning up the mess.

It was not long after this that Dad had finally had enough. He was determined not be beaten by the bears. That was the end to the beautiful sod roof that you see on the cabin on the cover photo.

It was replaced with a brown tin roof. This was the end of our bear break-ins.

In the bigger picture of things it had also become necessary due to the enormous amount of weight the roof was bearing. Over the many years the sod had become a replica of the surrounding ground cover. Everything from grasses to brush to small trees had begun to grow up there. It was only a matter of time before it became too much and gave way to the enormous weight. Leakage had also become an increasing problem along with the compound issue of snow. This obviously forever changed the look of the cabin but added many years of life to the structure.

One Last Tale

Last year while on a high alpine mule deer hunt in the Pasayten Wilderness area in northern Washington I had an opportunity to harvest my first bear. This was simply an opportunity I could not pass up. I came face to face with a black bear that had the coloring of a grizzly. It was either him or me. I chose him. He had a beautiful coat for a Cinnamon Bear. This had been my first close encounter with a black bear while hunting. They are normally very nocturnal and not seen during the day. I have to say I was quite proud of my first bear, even though it was not a large bear; it was a trophy to me. We had fresh bear steaks that night on the fire and a great story for the kids.

Brian's Bear 9/07

Chapter 15
Guest Times

"Friendship is unnecessary, like philosophy, like art.
It has no survival value; rather it is one of those things
that give value to survival."
-C.S. Lewis

Part I – The Horacek Brothers

Living in Alaska was like living in another country. It was on everyone's list to visit at least once. From my earliest memories as a child, my parents would invite visitors from the lower 48 states. I suppose the fact that Dad had moved his family to Alaska was part of the reason. The other part would have to be the sheer beauty and experience of visiting and experiencing Alaska. The fact that we had built this log cabin on a river, never really occurred to me as unique. Didn't everyone have a cabin and love to fish? As I grew I would find how unique we were in the big picture of family and friends scattered across the country.

My earliest memory of Dad sharing his new-found passion was when he invited his brother Pete and a friend of his to come up to Alaska and visit. Pete was still a young man just getting out of college and open to adventure. He made the drive all the way up from Nebraska in an old Jeep. I remember Dad being excited to take his brother fishing for kings. I was eager to join them but was disappointed to find out that this was not a trip I was to accompany them on. I was only seven at the time. I liked my Uncle Pete. He took my brother and me fishing to a nearby stream that unfortunately didn't have any fish in it since it was only glacier runoff and not habitable for fish. It didn't matter to us as we were just excited to get to go. I remember him buying me my first pocket knife. Boy, was I proud. I'm not sure my mom appreciated it that much, but Dad was fine with it so I got to keep it. It was a black simulated stag folder with two blades on one side and a smaller blade and bottle opener on the other. I still have it to this day on a shelf in my office.

Dad took Pete and his friend up to the mouth of Clear Creek and they camped on the big sand bar. The kings were running and there were no other fishermen there except them. This would be an absolute rarity and anomaly today as it would be hard not to count at least a hundred people there at this time of year.

Since I was not there I can only tell you that they had a great time and came home with many stories and FISH. This was a first for my dad, too. Mom had no idea what she was in for when they returned from their trip. They brought back some of the biggest kings we have ever seen come out of that area. They had left the heads and tails on, for what reason I do not know other than to show us kids how big they really were. These fish were so big that the only place to put them was the bathtub! I remember seeing several large king salmon lying in our bathtub. They stretched out the entire length of the tub. Dad made sure to take a few pictures with my mom holding them up in front of our house for her Tulsa friends and family.

My brother Scott and Mom holding one of Pete's king salmon in front of our house in Anchorage. ~1972

That trip was the starting point. Once we had our cabin built and a place for guests to actually stay, things would never be the same. I think word spread and it was a regular part of our lives to have guests from out of state come to Alaska. They did not come for the regular tourist experience.

They came to see and experience Dad's cabin and the fishing. It was not uncommon to have two or three different parties of people come up during the summer. Dad was not the kind of person who could easily say no. Once people had the opportunity to experience a week at the cabin, it would become a semi-regular event.

People were important to Dad. He liked sharing his experience and providing experiences for people that he knew they would not normally have. Dad had three brothers so many times it was one or more of them making the trip up to Alaska. Dad's older brother Perry, a respected and accomplished architect in Lawton, Oklahoma, soon became a regular. Perry had five kids like Dad and two of them were boys about the same age as me. In fact one of my cousins, John, was born on the same day and year as I was. Together with his brother Jeff who is now an internist in Portland, Oregon, they made several memorable trips to the cabin. There is nothing like a couple of Oklahoma crappie-catching boys tearing into a king salmon. Though many memories were made on the banks of the river, we all enjoyed the time at the cabin and around the campfire the most.

My Uncle Perry loved to nap. I think I have more pictures of Perry napping than catching fish. It is not that he didn't catch fish; he just became well known for both.

Perry catching some z's in the warm Alaska sunshine

Perry usually brought a full contingent of friends with him to the cabin. Whether neighbor, son-in-law, or his sons, we always had a cabin full from Oklahoma. One year he brought Dr. Richard Allgood, a thoracic surgeon. Another time son-in-law Rodney and his brother from Texas. Longtime neighbor and friend Col. Frank Hawthorne also made the trip.

Perry recalled, "Frank, your Dad and I had some problems getting up the creek and got stuck on some rocks. Your dad had everyone get out of the boat to help free it. Frank lost his footing and fell in the creek. After we got on our way, Frank was so wet and cold your Dad pulled over on a gravel bar to start a fire for Frank to get warm and dry. He didn't want him to get hypothermia."

Perry reminded me of a story of a fish he caught that was somewhat unorthodox. While fishing his line became tangled and came off the spool to make a mess. He had already cast his "secret" fly into the river. While trying to un-tangle the mess, he noticed something was pulling his line out. He couldn't reel due to the tangled line so he dropped his pole in the creek and began to pull the line in by hand and was able to land a nice rainbow trout without the help of his rod or reel!

Dad 'n' Pete

I know that some of the finest times my dad ever had were being with all three of his brothers at his cabin. It didn't matter if it was raining or shining, they had the rare opportunity to be together. Memories for a lifetime were made there.

The Horacek Brothers in front of the famous Talkeetna Grocery and Liquor Store, circa- 1986
Jerry, Pete, Perry, & Chuck

Likewise, some of my best memories were made from these trips, too. The fishing bug ran deep in the Horacek family and having the chance to fish with my cousins was always a thrill.

The Horacek Boys, Jeff, me, John, and Chris.

*Tent, handling
the overflow*

*"El Capitán" Retired Captain, U.S.
Navy, Jerry Horacek, commanding the
fire pit crew. - circa 1987*

Dad, Perry and Frank - circa 1985

*Frank, Perry, and me with a nice
string of silver salmon- circa 1985*

*John Horacek with a nice
silver salmon*

*Jeff Horacek with a large
Chum salmon*

I am not sure exactly how many trips we made to the cabin together but there were many. I was in college at this time with my cousins in Oklahoma. We were all fraternity brothers and more like real brothers than cousins.

Space at the cabin was at a premium when there were this many people. Many times we would have to improvise by pitching a tent or two to help accommodate everyone. The logistics of getting all the gear, food, and people to the cabin were a challenge. Dad just took it all in stride as he did everything else in life. Most of his time was spent shuttling people up and down the river. He always made sure they were in the best fishing hole.

My cousin Jeff Horacek made the most trips out of the clan to the cabin. Many times he would travel there alone just to get away and enjoy the fishing and time relaxing. I know that he probably has enough stories of his own from these trips to write a whole book himself.

Part II - Other Guests

Dad had an old high school mate named Jim who had invited a neighbor of his, Hank, to go with him to Alaska to go fishing. Dad had planned to take them up to the cabin during the salmon run and show these California guys some real fishing.

Chris, Jeff, and John Horacek enjoying their favorite fishing hole

I had the opportunity to sometimes accompany my dad with his guests and have some fond memories of fishing with Hank and Jim.

Jim Marshal and Hank Smith enjoying the cabin

Hank was a great guy who loved to fish. My Dad always enjoyed when Hank and Jim made a trip up to Alaska. I spoke to Hank on the phone about some of his memories at the cabin. He told me that they were all good memories and that he didn't have any particular ones that stood out to him. Hank turned 80 this year but had the opportunity to take his son Mark up to Alaska in 2005 fishing with Dad the week after I had my family up there. Neither of us knew that was our last time with Dad. Hank recalled how Dad was just not himself that year.

He did remind me of the time Dad noticed that the boat was not tied up in front of the cabin where it should have been and was floating down the river with no one in it. He remembered running down the side of the river bank with me to catch the boat before it got too far away. I had forgot all about that until Hank reminded me, but I can see why that might have left an impression.

Captain Chuck and Hank Smith

Hank also recalled that the same thing happened on another trip to the cabin. While he was fishing with Jim and Dad at Fish Creek, the boat got loose and floated down nearly to the mouth of the creek where it joins the Talkeetna River. Luckily, Dad got a ride down the creek to retrieve his boat. Memories like these make great campfire stories.

Hank was more of what you might call a purist when it came to fishing. He was an experienced fly fisherman and had all the nice rods and reels and gear you could imagine. Hank recalled in our conversation how Dad would take out his old clunker of a reel with 30 lb. test line and an old salmon rod with a broken tip and still catch more fish than the both of them.

Hank said he still pictures Dad smiling, easy going, and always hospitable.

Dad was best man in Jim's wedding. They stayed in touch over the years. Dad invited Jim to go fishing to Alaska in the mid 1980's and over the years Jim made about five trips there with Hank. Jim is now retired from sales in commercial office furniture and lives in Austin, Texas.

He remembered when he first went up to the cabin with Dad. He thought the shotgun and .357 Magnum in the boat were just for show or something. Then when they got to the cabin and Dad wouldn't let him get out of the boat until he did his customary "bear check," he soon realized that it might not be for just show after all. The first time Jim wanted to walk up the trail from the cabin to go do some fishing upstream, Dad asked Jim if he was going to take the shotgun with him. Jim said he laughed it off and then agreed he would take the pistol because it was lighter and easier to carry. Dad said, "Jim, you know what that's good for don't you? If you run into a griz you can shoot yourself." Then it was Dad's turn for a laugh. Dad was always joking around like that. He had fun with the unexperienced out-of-towners as we called them.

Jim reminded me of a story about his first encounter with a bear at the cabin. They were in the cabin sitting at the table eating dinner when a black bear came walking by the front of the cabin. Jim told Dad what he just saw and Dad got his shotgun ready. The bear walked by the side of the cabin toward the back so Dad opened the door and slowly walked out. His plan was to just shoot a cracker round at the bear to scare him off. As he walked around the corner, closely followed by Jim and Hank, he saw the bear about 30 feet away. Dad carefully aimed and shot. I am not sure if he forgot what he was shooting at that moment but I am sure he very quickly figured it out. The cracker round hit the bear, bounced off of him, and rebounded back towards Dad, Jim, and Hank and exploded! They went running one way and the bear the other!

I know that I feel somewhat remiss about not including all the people that have visited the cabin with Dad over the years. There were many friends and old classmates from both Mom's and Dad's past. There were exchange students from Germany, hockey players from Minnesota, work friends and their families, neighbor kids, and friends of mine and of all my siblings. I am sure each one would have many funny stories of their own to share.

Dad was always very patient and understanding with his guests. He never made anyone feel unwelcome. When it came to gas and food, Dad would always pay, or try to pay. If anyone wanted to help or chip in, that was fine. He provided all the gear he could from tackle to life vests to raingear and toilet paper. No one went without having a good time no matter the weather conditions or fishing conditions. It was always a good time for all. That is the only way Dad would have wanted it. He always wanted to provide a trip that they would enjoy and remember. He was simply the hotel for the night before, the driver, the captain, the camp host, the fishing guide, cook, and most of all, friend.

Chapter 16
High Waters II

"I have never seen a river that I could not love. Moving water has a fascinating vitality. It has power and grace and associations. It has a thousand colors and a thousand shapes, yet it follows laws so definite that the tiniest streamlet is an exact replica of a great river."
-Roderick Haig Brown

Part 1: Another 50 feet gone!

Dad's passing had been hard on all. It seemed life at the cabin would never be the same. During that first summer in 2006 without Dad, I had planned not to go to the cabin. This would be the first summer I did not travel back to Alaska. It was a long hard summer for me. I wasn't sure how long it would be before I made it back there. I did, however, have my friends I planned to take back there, fishing, and knew I couldn't stay away for long.

Dad chose to be cremated and wanted his ashes to be spread at the cabin. This meant getting together with the rest of the family at the cabin sometime during the summer or fall. Due to various scheduling issues we had not been able to get everyone there at the same time. That was soon to change.

On August 19, I received an e-mail from my mom along with the NOAA report for the Talkeetna River and nearby drainage areas. It was not good news. The report said many of the rivers and streams in the area where expected to be at or above flood stage within the next 24 hours. Mom lamented on what that could mean for us and our need to be together as a family during this time. Worried about the cabin and what could possibly happen, we had to just wait and see what the outcome would be. The report expected the Talkeetna River to peak at or above 12 feet. That was not good news. It was only a short 20 years ago that the river was that high. I thought to myself, "There is no way it could ever flood as bad as it did back then, could it?" After all we had moved the cabin back to a safe distance. There was nothing I could do about it. I felt helpless and did not sleep well that night.

We anxiously waited for the news about the water and conditions on the creek. Several of our neighbors had access to planes and would check as soon as the weather cleared and presented better flying conditions. On August 21, I received an e-mail with aerial photos taken by our good friend Dan Pavey. My eyes could not believe what I saw in those photos. They showed a very full, chocolate-colored river flowing very deep and wide, right in front of our cabin.

The almost unthinkable had happened, again! The corner of the cabin laid hanging over the bank of the river just as it did 20 years ago! Almost the exact same thing happened. The river had

Aerial photo of the 2006 Clear Creek flood - Photo by Dan Pavey
The end of the fallen tree is where the bank was.

swollen so much and had such force that it literally carved out and took over 50 feet of land in front of our cabin. The front porch did not even survive this time. It was ripped off and swept away. It is a wonder how the river managed to come that close without taking my dad's beloved cabin away. The pictures were a little hard to make out. It was not until I received some photos from the vantage point of the river that I was able to see the full impact. I knew I needed to get up there soon to help save our cabin.

It wasn't until the end of the month that plans were finalized. I would make the trip with my son Jaeden who was only nine and accompany my brother Chris and sister Carrie. Arrangements had been made with Dan Pavey, our longtime friend and neighbor, to do the initial damage assessment and preparations to eventually move our cabin again. Dan had been a part of the original team of engineers and men that rallied to help Dad in October, 1986. Dan was a respected geologist and craftsman we would rely on heavily for support and guidance through this process.

My brother, Chris, happened to work for the largest lumber store in the state and had access to all the lumber we would need. Through his careful preparations, we would have all the supplies we needed and more. Things would be different this time. We did not have the numbers of people as before but with the help of technology, we were able to do things more efficiently than my Dad had done. They had relied on their numbers; we would rely on our planning.

During the summer my mom made plans to purchase a new boat. One that would have the power and grace that we never had before. Dad's old boat was sold and through much research and input from Dan, Mom purchased what we thought would be the boat for the next generation. Dan helped test it and make sure it was ready for its inaugural voyage to the cabin. There were so many unknowns taking a new boat up the river. How would it perform? Could it handle the loads? What if it didn't? As it worked out, I was going to be the one to take it up the first time. My brother, Chris, was not able to go until the next day. Dan met us at the boat launch and we loaded and set out. I had to get a feel for how the boat performed, so after launching, we ran downstream near the launch to make a short run up river and make sure all was well. It certainly had the power we needed and was very quick to respond turning. I was a little nervous with my young son on board and Mom. It had been a long time, in fact many years, since I had driven the river by myself. Dad was always the pilot and captain. I realized that it was now my time to step up.

The trip up the Talkeetna went well. I was surprised at how much it had changed. We took a new channel that we had never used before because the flood had opened it up to passage and had cleared many of the fallen trees that used to line the banks and block parts of the channel.

When we approached Clear Creek, there were many fishermen already at the mouth. It was silver salmon season and despite the flood having ravaged the river, the people still managed to make it up there to fish. There was only a narrow channel flowing out the mouth with a large shallow rock bar to the left. We could only slow for a moment and then had to power up through the narrow chute of water to avoid hitting rocks. People on the bank just don't understand this and think that we are somehow being rude by not going slow while they fish. Many showed us the international sign of dislike with their finger but my eyes were on the rocks and making sure I followed directly where Dan went. There were many new rock bars and shallows that had not been there in years past. I followed Dan's boat closely, almost too closely at times, and found myself only several feet away from his transom. I didn't want to miss a turn, rock, or tree that he avoided.

As we rounded the final bend, I was able to see the cabin for the first time. I pulled up to the bank and we tied off the boat. Dan continued up the river to his cabin. He would return tomorrow to go back down with me for our lumber, supplies, and my brother and nephew. As I exited the boat, I was amazed at what I saw. Where there once was a fire pit was a 10-foot sheer drop into the river. The fire pit area was actually out in the middle of what was now the channel of the creek. The rock bar on the far side was now much bigger and stretched out over toward our side of the creek. Many new rocks lay up above the water level that had never been there. It was clear that the other side of the creek gained as much land as we had lost. As I looked at the cabin, I saw that it was actually hanging over the bank more so than it had back in '86. A small ramp was required to reach the front door. It was clear that this was going to be a very challenging task.

What the cabin looked like the day we arrived

That first night was spent contemplating and surveying the area behind the cabin. As I walked through the grass I made note of the trees that would have to be cut down providing an open path to move the cabin. There was only about 100 feet of available property back to the base of a small but steep hill. My dad had often talked about the fact that, if he had to do it all over again, he would have built at the base of the hill. It was a safe distance back away from the river and provided more cover from boats and passers-by on the river.

There were no fewer than half a dozen trees. Many of them were several feet in circumference. These would be used for more than firewood. They would provide the rollers for the cabin to be moved. Then there were the stumps to deal with. They would have to be cleared somehow. I wondered how the pioneers of old dealt with this. They had mules and horses and probably burned them. That's what we would do, burn them out. There was a nice spot near the base of the hill that was free from trees and had level ground. I spent some time daydreaming of what it would look like being back that far from the river. Wondering just how hard it would be to move it ourselves.

The edge of the riverbank told a story of the river long ago. It was clear that the very ground the cabin was on was once the river bed. Layers of silt and smooth rocks could be seen showing how the river had one day flooded and deposited the existing ground. I found it amazing that so much could be seen from a newly carved river bank.

The water level in front of the cabin used to be fairly shallow. One could cross with hip waders if needed. Where the fire pit once stood, is now a deep hole. The river seemingly dug out the area and from the top looking down, I am not able to see the bottom.

The fire pit was located just right of where I stand, the water now too deep to even wade. The many layers of old river rock can be seen with the layers of silt deposited on top from many years ago when the river once ran there.

The next day I went down the river with Dan to pick up my brother Chris and nephew Anthony at the boat launch. They were pulling a trailer loaded with wood. Chris had procured some very large 6x8x20-feet long timbers as well as plenty of 6x8x3-feet blocks. The task of loading this heavy timber in the boats would prove to be a challenge. Dan made sure each boat was sufficiently balanced and the weight properly distributed. It was still not known how the boats would perform carrying a load like this up the river.

Once loaded we headed upstream. I was surprised how well things worked and we managed to not hit any rocks despite the falling level of the rivers. After arriving, we had to then unload these heavy timbers and place them where they would soon be needed. The blocks were all stacked in back of the cabin, staged to provide easy access for the initial project of jacking and blocking the cabin.

Large timber delicately balanced in Dan's boat

The cabin needed to be raised about 2 feet higher than its present level. This was a delicate and slow process. A hole had to be dug about 2 feet deep under each corner. Large blocks were then placed in the hole to allow a level and stable place for the jacks. The cabin then needed to be hand jacked a few inches at a time. After each jacking, a new block was placed to keep the cabin at that slightly new level.

The cabin was old and in much worse shape than the last time it was moved. The bottom logs were mostly rotted from the years of dampness on the ground. The timber and jack would sometimes just compress right into them. The weather was quite warm and the work was hard. We dug and jacked and dug and jacked until we had the whole cabin standing on blocks.

Chris and Dan access the jack under the left front corner

The next step was a tricky one. We had decided that since the logs were too weak on the bottom we would place the long timbers all the way under the cabin to act as skids. These would then be strapped and bolted with metal brackets to the solid logs above. Through this process Mom was busily cleaning and organizing in the cabin. It would creak and pop as it was being jacked, occasionally startling Mom and prompting her to stick her head out to inquire what was going on. The blocking process took us almost three days. Dan had been a huge help and provided a pneumatic jack that ran off an old generator he had. This was used in addition to the small hand-cranked bottle jack we had.

Cabin now blocked up to a height of 2 feet

Trees were then cut and placed in position around the cabin. Soon it was almost ready for moving but that would have to happen next summer as winter was just around the bend and with the river falling, it would soon be too shallow for our boats to run.

Large logs being placed under the cabin to use as rollers

Would it stand through the next winter? What if the spring floods proved to be bad and just took a little more land? The cabin would literally disappear without a trace; forever gone into the grasp of the mighty river it had stood watch over all these years.

Part 2: The Big Move

The cabin now on "roller logs" and ready to be moved

Plans were made for another major work trip to the cabin the following summer. This time we would be joined by my brother Scott. We had only a short window of time due to schedules and the fact that my brother Chris had his second set of twin boys at home now with his wife Jen. My son Jaeden would once again make the trek with me and spend most of his time with his Auntie Carrie, fishing and playing like most 10 year olds want to do.

This trip would center on finishing preparing the cabin for the big move. There was still much work to do. Chris and I got a start on the details while we waited for Scott to join us. We carefully wrapped 3/8-inch steel cabling around the whole cabin, twice, and then ran it back to the location of the winches that were anchored to a tree about 50 yards straight behind the cabin. The cabin would have to be moved with nothing more than a large hand-cranked winch.

We were not sure how well this would work, or if it would work at all. The best of planning and engineering went into all the preparations we made. The rest was out of our hands or really totally left to our hands.

Scott proved to be a big help with fastening the cables and rigging. We then began the rigorous task of cranking the winch. The winch was not your normal winch. We had to anchor it to a tree and figure out a way to suspend it in the air to provide a direct path to the level of the cable on the cabin. We cut a small 6-inch pine tree off to a height of about 4 feet. The winch was then lifted up onto the tree and balanced until the crank had tightened the slack in the cable and the winch would then be suspended above the ground. One person could crank the winch but that proved to be just too much work so we decided to create shifts. One man watched the cable and the cabin, measured the progress, and the other two would crank.

The cabin creaked loudly as the tension in the cable tightened. Then with a sudden jump, it popped forward about 4 inches. We were so excited we stopped to take pictures of our progress. Surely we can get this done I thought to myself.

Between turns we had to rest, replace logs that were acting as giant rollers for the cabin, and then it was back to cranking. We were only able to do about 20 rotations a turn before collapsing with exhaustion. That would gain us 3-4 inches of movement. Our goal for the weekend was adjusted after realizing how hard this was going to be. We set out originally to move the cabin at least 25 feet this weekend. That was soon changed to maybe 15-20 feet, depending on how long we could last.

Back of the cabin with cables running back to a tree near the jack, just like the photo from 1986

I lamented at not being able to spend the time fishing with my 10-year-old son. He was a good sport and knew that we were there to work. It was hard for him, though, knowing that there was a river jammed full of salmon and not having much time to fish. Jaeden managed to find projects to help. He helped gather wood for the new temporary fire pit, stack blocks, and dig a new set of earthen stairs up the bank. He still managed to fish on his own and caught many salmon right out of the boat in front of the cabin.

Late in the afternoon we sat in the shade on the bank watching a grizzly far downstream make his way slowly up the rock bar across from us. Eventually he was directly across from us, all the while searching the shore for an easy meal. I thought he must have been a young bear or a lazy bear as he never ventured out into the water where there were plenty of fish.

Instead he settled for a dead rotting fish on the bank. He stopped and literally sat down on his bottom as he ate what was left of the salmon and then meandered on his way up stream. He never saw us nor paid any attention to what was directly across from him. It was a great experience to share with my son to see a wild grizzly so close and be able to watch him as we did.

My son Jaeden fishing out of the boat in front of the cabin on a warm summer day

We were able to move the cabin back successfully around 20 feet

Jaeden would end up convincing me to stay the whole week with my sister at her cabin up on the hill so he could fish and enjoy the cabin life. I was somewhat apprehensive because of the bears. But in the end I agreed and he ended up having the fun of a lifetime with many great memories to share. He caught around ten silver salmon, saw more bears, and got to shoot guns with the big boys.

We managed to get the cabin back about 20 feet before having to call it quits. Once again it would have to wait until next year to be finished and put in its final resting place. I was much more relieved, knowing we had moved it back to a safe distance, at least I hoped, so that I would not have to worry about loosing it. I would have to return once again for a work trip to get the job finished.

Front lawn

All of the land seen in this photo is no longer there, it was washed away in the flood.

Chapter 17
The Legacy

leg·a·cy, n., pl. –cies
Something handed down from an ancestor or a
predecessor or from the past:

"The Sun shines not on us but in us.
The Rivers flow not past, But through us."
-John Muir

Every story must have an ending. This is one story that has not yet ended and yet I must find a place to at least conclude this chapter. I set out on a journey to try to tell a story about a man who was very dear to me. A man who had a dream that he saw come to fruition and a man who shared that dream with anyone he could.

The cabin he built was not a temple, not a home, not even a nice cabin but it was as close to holy ground as my dad would ever get. He had a passion and a desire for all that the outdoors had to offer. This book is merely one way that I could find to honor him and his memory to all of his family and friends and especially those who had the honor to share it with him.

I don't know what my dad would have done differently had he been here for the last flood but I do know that he would be proud of us for coming together as a family as best we could to help preserve his memories and life at our family cabin. Some may think that it is silly and that we should have just let nature take its course and carry that old thing away. I, however, could not find it in myself to consider that. Not after what I had experienced there and all the memories that spin round my head on days I dream of nothing more than just to have a weekend at the cabin. Living in Seattle with my family makes it difficult for me to get there more than maybe once a year. Yet that is in itself so satisfying as to tide me over just enough for the next year.

I want my children to share and have some of the same experiences I did. To know what it is like to battle the elements and challenge the river to get to a small piece of heaven on earth. It will never be the same without my dad but nothing lasts forever and as long as I am able, I will do all I can to see that the legacy my father started is carried on.

The summer of 2004, after having spent time at the cabin fishing with the guys, I decided to also take my family up to the cabin so they could have that experience and memories. I knew that Dad was not doing well and really wanted this time with him.

As things turned out, we were unable to get up Clear Creek because the water level was so low and it made it impossible with his large boat. We were forced to use the campground at the boat launch in Talkeetna. Dad brought up the motor home and we stayed the nights there and spent the day out on the river fishing. This was the first real attempt for my kids to get to catch a salmon.

My wife had also not fished for quite a long time and I was anxious to watch her catch a fish.

Dad with his granddaughter Talia and grandson Jaeden on what was their last trip up the river with their Grandpa

This turned out to be a very special time for the kids with their grandfather. They had a ball fishing and playing along the river. The sight of seeing my then 4-year old daughter stand in the freezing water in her bare feet, undistracted as she learned to master a full size salmon rod with an open-face spinning reel. Grandpa loved watching that and I think for one of the first times, really had some time to connect with his grandkids who only are able to see him once a year.

Dad giving Talia some fishing tips

*The next generation of Horaceks
learning how to fish*

My wife, Kim, turned out to be the lucky angler that day and caught a real nice silver salmon with the kids. I did not know at the time that this would be their last time to see their grandpa and to fish with him. They truly represent the next generation of our family and have a share in this legacy.

I suppose we will ultimately get the cabin moved and settled into its new spot back by the hill. It is in need of much repair and attention that is now proving to be harder and harder to provide.

The greatest challenge still remains, the never-ending force of the river and all that goes with it.

The water levels are more of a problem than ever before due to new rock bars and shallow areas of the river. More people are using quads or four-wheelers to cross the back county rather than run the river. It is partially due to the ability to get access when the river is low and the cost factor of maintaining and running a river boat.

We would like to build a new cabin on the property for the next generation to enjoy and maybe use the old cabin as a bunk house. My sister Carrie has her own cabin now and doesn't really have the need for it. My brother Chris has four boys who some day will be old enough to enjoy going to the cabin so I am hoping that will help ensure the long term viability of its existence for their sake and ours.

Part of me has the desire and dream of one day returning to Alaska and being able to share in the experience and pleasure of utilizing the cabin. My mom is not able to go there without someone taking her and has found that it is going to be much less common than in the past when it was used each weekend by my dad. So only time will tell the ultimate future of the cabin. As for the river that provides the beauty and sustenance of all the surrounding trees and animals, I suspect that it will continue on its never-ending path of forever changing the landscape and area surrounding it.

Dad laid the foundation for us to follow. He showed us the way and taught us how to handle the obstacles we would encounter along the way. It is through his undying love and patience that we are able to continue to wear his mantel as best as God enables us.

*"The song of the river ends not at her banks, but in the hearts of
those who have loved her."*
~Buffalo Joe

Searching the Wilds

Searching the wilds, remote and full of mystique,
One ponders the reasons to seek that which is unique.

Is it the quiet, whispers of breezes,
kisses of direct or diffused light,
Nature in stillness or in song,
Is it the feeling that settles, All is right and well
and nothing's wrong?
Is it the communion with creation and life free upon the range?
Is it a feeling, or just the brief trip through millenniums of time?
Is it the stretches of earth seldom, if ever, walked by man,
Changes of seasons short and long, shrouds of snow in
blizzards or drift, washes of heavy or drizzling rains?
Is it the quest for game, trophies, or meat or is it a quest for
treasures, some black and fluid, some just called Gold?

Is it the need to be up high, to survey the world, or
To be nestled securely among forests' tall trees, branches
outspread to gentle the winds and soften the rains that pat on
tent, tarp, roofs of tin.

Is it any of the above, mentioned herein,
Is it about where one is going, or where one's hopes have been?

The answer is simple, or so we are told,
It's the experience one is driven and destined to hold.
It's in the seeking, in the search, and just simply the Quest.
It's all the above, all these things and more.
In the remote we are only a guest,
the answer here, is simply yes!

~ L. A. Horacek

About the Author

Brian grew up in Anchorage, Alaska. His dad introduced him to the outdoors at an early age. Fishing and hunting were a regular part of his life. His dad started by taking him and his brother fishing to many local lakes and streams and hunting for snowshoe rabbits as early as 7 years old. Each fall the first week of school was always missed due to the start of the hunting season when he and his dad and brother would go on a weeklong hunting trip somewhere in the  interior of Alaska. Many of the essential skills of surviving in the wilderness were learned on these trips. The author also had first hand experience at the age of 13 and 14 helping his father build a log cabin on their property in Talkeetna, Alaska.

Brian graduated from Oklahoma State University with a B.S. in International Business Management. Brian moved to the Seattle, Washington area to pursue a career in sales.

The respect and passion for the outdoors runs deep in his family and is a big part of Brian's life. He too spends much time with his family hiking, camping, fishing and hunting in the Washington state area while making regular trips to Alaska to fish and visit the family cabin.

Brian's dad was diagnosed with cancer in December of 2004 shortly after the fishing trip he took to the family cabin discussed in this book. His dad battled the cancer bravely for nearly a year and passed in November of 2005.

This book is his legacy.

Quick Order Form

Email orders: orders@clearcreekpub.com
Fax orders: 425-645-8058 Send this form
Telephone orders: 425-379-9068 *Have your credit card ready.*

Postal orders:
Clear Creek Publications, Brian Horacek
16212 Bothell Everett Hwy. , Suite F151
Mill Creek, WA 98012

Please send _____ book(s) at $16.99 per copy.
I understand that I may return them for a full refund, for any reason, no questions asked.

Name: _____

Address: _____

City: _____ State: _____ Zip: _____

Telephone: _____

Email Address: _____

Sales Tax: Please add 8.6% for products shipped to Washington state addresses.

Shipping: Please select:
☐ Air - Please add $6.00
☐ Ground - Please add $3.00
☐ International - Please add $10.00

Payment:
☐ Check ☐ Credit Card
☐ Visa ☐ Mastercard
☐ Amex ☐ Discover

Card Number: _____

Name on Card: _____ Exp. Date _____